Teaching Science in a Multicultural World

by Dr. Elizabeth Rhodes Offutt

Fearon Teacher Aids

ACKNOWLEDGMENTS

I would like to thank several individuals for their help and support: my husband, Charles Offutt; Sheri Lott, my graduate assistant; Allison Rotch, my student assistant; and members of the faculty and staff in the School of Education at Samford University for their encouragement, ideas, and support.

Executive Editor: Jeri Cipriano
Editor: Jeanne Gleason

 FEARON TEACHER AIDS
An Imprint of Modern Curriculum
A Division of Simon & Schuster
299 Jefferson Road, P.O. Box 480
Parsippany, NJ 07054-0480

1 2 3 4 5 6 7 8 9   MAL   01 00 99 98 97 96

Contents

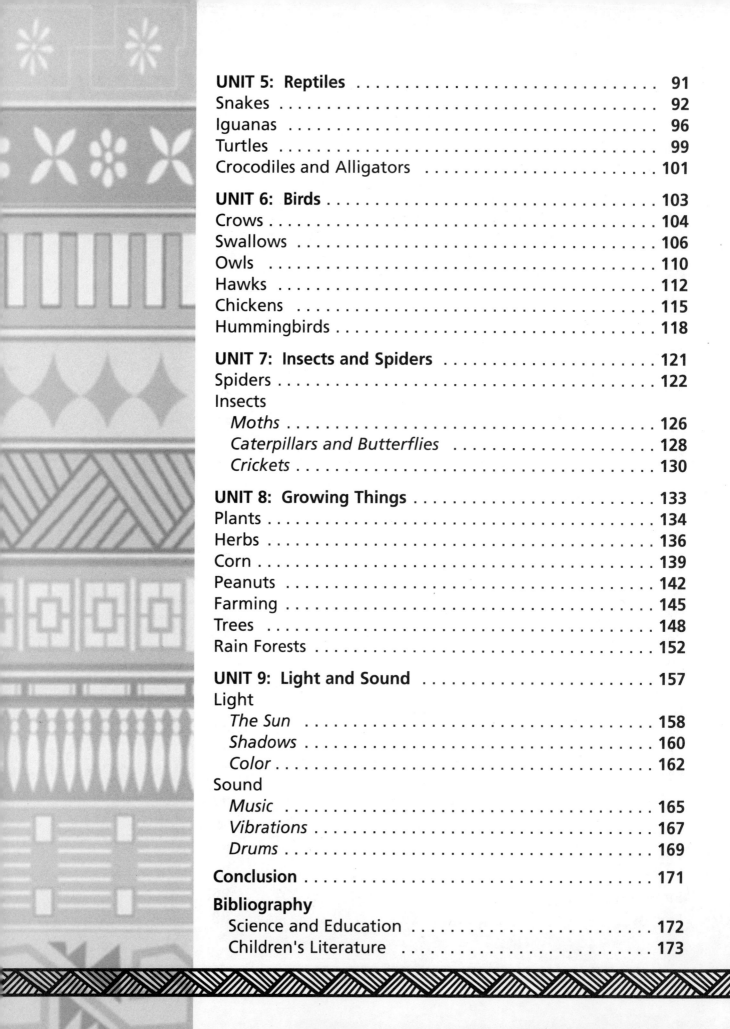

Every child has a family heritage to learn about. Connecting heritage and culture with each child may be one key to improving not only science instruction but increasing understanding of ourselves within our complex and interconnected world. Each culture has its own characteristic science because of the unique application of basic processes, such as observing, predicting, and explaining events in the world. People throughout the world have developed different ways of interacting and understanding the natural world because they have lived in different environments. These different environments have presented different problems to solve.

Using multicultural children's literature to teach science concepts provides many unique and valuable educational, social, and cultural benefits. Cultural connections for children of different ethnic backgrounds can be encouraged. The cultural heritage of children can come alive at school in all subject areas.

Throughout this book, information about the achievements of different cultures will be presented in a box with the title *Ethnoscience Fact.*

Introduction

ETHNO SCIENCE FACT

Ethnoscience is an awareness of a culture's contribution to the scientific disciplines.

Children can begin to understand difficult and complex concepts through the use of stimulating and interesting stories. They can obtain new insights when they realize how science fits into the everyday life of people throughout the world. Many subject areas can be integrated through the use of motivating, stimulating, and exciting stories.

There is a growing body of evidence that links multicultural education and improved academic learning. With the use of children's literature, the elementary educator can begin to integrate multicultural connections within the science curriculum. The challenge and key to successful integration is to find authentic nonstereotypical stories that capture the essence of the culture.

Using this approach, it would be beyond the scope of this resource book to discuss the vast number of curriculum possibilities for each science concept. Several major concepts will be discussed within the context of emphasizing multicultural literature and integrating science activities.

Benjamin Banneker (1731–1806) published a series of almanacs containing scientific information. These almanacs were the first scientific books written by an African American.

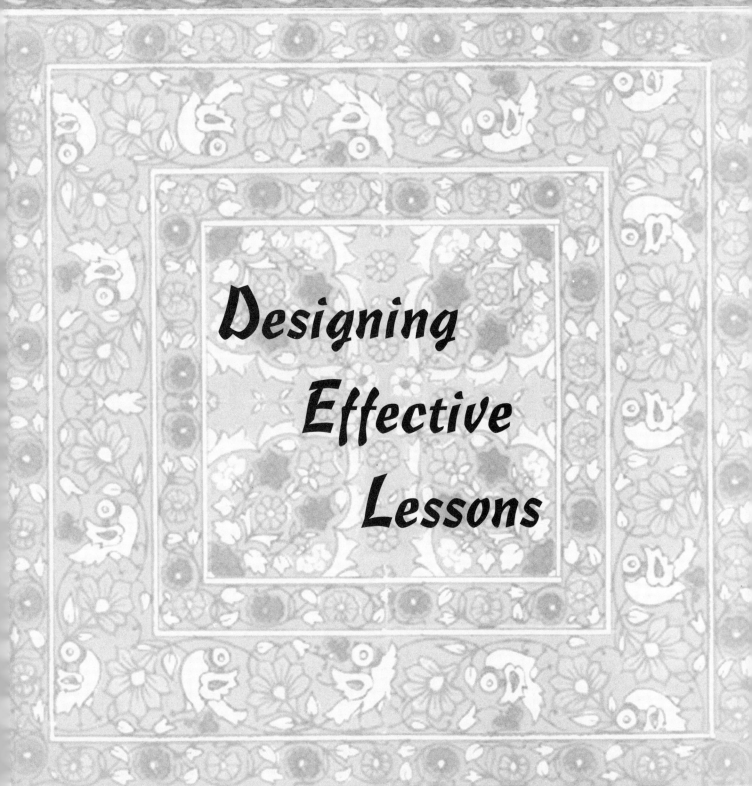

Designing Effective Lessons

Designing Effective Lessons

Scientific Processes

The purpose of teaching science in the elementary school is to provide children with the opportunity to develop special tools. These special tools are the scientific processes that will help them become problem solvers. Science process skills are at the heart of what learning is all about. Multicultural children's literature can be used as a vehicle to teach children more about science concepts. The ultimate goal in science instruction is to provide children with many opportunities throughout each lesson to develop at least one or more processes by using scientific inquiry.

Scientific inquiry is a search for truth and knowledge. If you are scientific, you are able to identify problems, make educated guesses or hypotheses, and investigate them. Scientists have these abilities. Acting like a scientist means using these attitudes and processes.

What are these processes? There are many, but the following list contains a few of the most important ones children need to practice in order to become effective problem solvers.

Connecting

To discover concepts through a personal understanding of relationships. Students can become inspired when they feel a deep connectedness with what is being taught. If students do not find a task, project, or assignment meaningful they will not be motivated to ask questions and find the answers to those questions.

Thinking

Students should be encouraged to become creative thinkers. They should not view the teacher as the only authority and source of knowledge in the classroom. Teachers need to help children construct their own personal way of solving problems, rather than tell them how they should solve the problem.

Questioning

Students have a natural curiosity. As small children, they are full of endless questions. This is a wonderful ability. Teachers should take care not to stifle or suppress students' questions. Students need to feel confident that they have the freedom to ask questions about what they experience in their everyday life. They need to know that they also have the ability to find a way to answer those questions.

Reading

Students need to recognize that reading is an integral part of science. Reading and science are thus interrelated and should be integrated throughout the instruction of both subject areas.

Observing

Observing is the process by which youngsters use their senses to identify objects and their properties. Using their senses, youngsters should be able to describe an object and any changes in the object or its properties. Observation is basic to all experiences in science, and youngsters are encouraged to develop this process to the fullest extent possible.

Hypothesizing and Predicting

To make predictions (guesses) based on data collected and then to test the predictions through the use of manipulative materials in personally designed experiments.

Experimenting

To involve youngsters in the process of experimentation. Youngsters identify and control variables that affect their hypothesis. This may involve abstract thinking, if several variables are involved. Students can perhaps begin with an experiment in which they just compare a control group with another experimental group with one variable. Eventually, they can learn methods to keep track of their identification process. Students need to view experiments as fun and exciting. An experiment can be viewed as a mystery to be solved by a detective.

Collecting and Analyzing Data

To record and organize data by analyzing information from a variety of sources. Children should be encouraged to think of creative ways to collect data. Graphing and charting their data in interesting and effective ways are vital to this process.

Estimating

To involve youngsters in the process of estimation and to describe how estimation is a useful practice in science; to introduce youngsters to the metric and standard systems of measurement. Children can also experiment with nonstandard units of measurement for estimation (their hands, paper clips, their arms, and so on).

Comparing

Children should be able to identify and compare variables within science concepts to see similarities and differences.

Measuring

To identify opportunities where estimates or accurate measurements are required and to understand procedures to use to find out the information needed.

Classifying

To demonstrate a method of sorting by properties, such as characteristics of skeletons, animal tracks, or rain forests.

Inferring

Inferences are ideas that have been refined through observation and testing. Students will learn that, the more observations they do, the more valid their inferences will be. It is exciting to watch as children develop this ability.

Testing and Evaluating

To review, test, and evaluate basic knowledge acquired through careful data collection, observations, and synthesis of information.

Reporting

To introduce students to computers, library resources, and other tools to use when doing research in science. Students can take information gathered through research and organize it to present to others in both written and oral communication.

Designing Effective Lessons

Cognitive Levels

In addition to making sure that scientific processes are taught in each lesson, it is important to become aware of the system of classifying educational objectives. This system described by Bloom* in 1956 has come to be identified as Bloom's Taxonomy. Teachers can use this classification system as a guide when designing lessons.

The following list can serve as a source of ideas about the various levels, and the types of activities can be encouraged in each one.

Knowledge

Definition: recalling, restating, and remembering learned information

Sample verbs used at this level: define, find, identify, label, list, locate, name, state, tell

Comprehension

Definition: grasping meaning of information by interpreting and translating learning

Sample verbs used at this level: conclude, contrast, describe, discuss, draw, explain, organize, report, restate, summarize

Application

Definition: making use of information in a context different from the one in which it was learned

Sample verbs used at this level: apply, classify, demonstrate, dramatize, experiment, illustrate, interpret, predict

* Bloom, B. *Taxonomy of Educational Objectives, Handbook I:* Cognitive Domain. New York: David McKay, 1956.

Analysis

Definition: breaking learned information into its component parts

Sample verbs used at this level: analyze, arrange, categorize, differentiate, discover, examine, solve, survey, transform

Synthesis

Definition: creating new information and ideas using previous learning

Sample verbs used at this level: construct, design, formulate, imagine, invent, plan, propose, suppose

Evaluation

Definition: making judgments about learned information on basis of established criteria

Sample verbs used at this level: argue, assess, conclude, defend, evaluate, judge, justify, rank, rate

Designing Effective Lessons

SAMPLE LESSON
Balloon Magic

LITERATURE

DuBois, W. *The Twenty-One Balloons.* New York: Puffin, 1975.

Professor Sherman sets sail in a giant balloon, determined to circumnavigate the globe.

BACKGROUND INFORMATION

Carbon dioxide is a gas that is heavier than air. It can be used to put out fires. A chemical change is a reaction that produces new substances.

Activity: Balloon Magic

Materials: (for each pair or group)

- 7-in. balloon
- 1 tablespoon of baking soda
- 3 oz. vinegar in a 10–12 oz. plastic bottle
- Plastic spoon

Ahead of time: *Measure out baking soda and vinegar. Blow up each balloon several times to stretch it.*

Give each pair of students (or group of students) a balloon. While one student stretches open the mouth of the balloon, another (using a plastic spoon) puts one tablespoon of baking soda inside. Next, have students carefully and slowly stretch the mouth of the balloon over the mouth of the bottle. Before going further, ask children to predict what will happen when the balloon is tipped over. After discussing various possibilities, allow students to lift up the balloon so that the baking soda falls into the vinegar.

Students will have fun observing. You should see bubbles in the bottle and the balloon inflating rapidly. A solid and a liquid were mixed together to produce a gas. The gas that is produced is carbon dioxide.

Processes Involved in Balloon Magic

- **Thinking** about ways to expand a balloon without blowing into it

- **Hypothesizing** and **Predicting** what will happen as the baking soda mixes with the vinegar

- **Observing** chemical changes

- **Questioning** the results and why they occurred

- **Testing** and **Evaluating** variations in this experiment by controlling and identifying variables, such as the amount of baking soda or vinegar

- **Demonstrating** a gas-collecting method

- **Making** scientific observations

- **Inferring** conclusions about the nature of creating gas as a result of observations and testing

- **Connecting** the scientific concept of chemical change with a personal experience

- **Measuring** amounts of baking soda and vinegar

Bloom's Cognitive Levels
Identified in the Sample Lesson

Knowledge

- Students can identify a solid, a liquid, and a gas in this experiment.
- Students can recall and restate the steps to do this experiment.
- Students can define what a chemical reaction is.

Comprehension

- Students can compare and contrast the air inside the bottle before and after the chemical reaction occurs.
- Students can explain what carbon dioxide is.
- Students can summarize how a chemical reaction occurs.

Application

- Students can predict what will happen when vinegar and baking soda mix in other types of projects or experiments.
- Students can manipulate variables (such as vinegar and baking soda) to produce different effects.

Analysis

- Students can analyze and discover the individual components of carbon dioxide.
- Students can transform a liquid and solid into another state.

Synthesis

- Students can make a chemical change to create a new project, which would benefit from a different source of energy (blowing up balloons using chemicals, not air).
- Students can experiment with other solids and liquids to produce new chemical changes.

Evaluation

- Students can conclude how chemical reactions occur.
- Students can evaluate various methods to create carbon dioxide.

Program Rationale

Curiosity is the most important characteristic a child can have. Children naturally are curious about everything they see, touch, and experience. Over time, however, many children become discouraged when teachers and parents become impatient with their questions or fail to give them a chance to find out the answers. If children are always told the answer to all they are curious about, they do not develop the ability to solve problems themselves.

We are preparing children for jobs that may not have been invented yet! Therefore, we need to focus on the skills necessary to prepare them to solve problems in any job they may encounter in their future. These skills require the development, practice, and review of the processes described.

Try to include at least one or more process in each lesson you do with students. Each of the activities in this book will give you opportunities to allow children to develop these processes. A teacher should be a guide—a fellow researcher with the children. Try not to answer all of children's questions. Try to encourage them to fully explore what they already know and find a way to discover what they do not know.

This book is not meant for teachers to give information to children. It is best utilized as a source of ideas and motivation to stir up the curiosity of children, provide opportunities to develop scientific processes, find out about cultures around the world, and explore many science concepts.

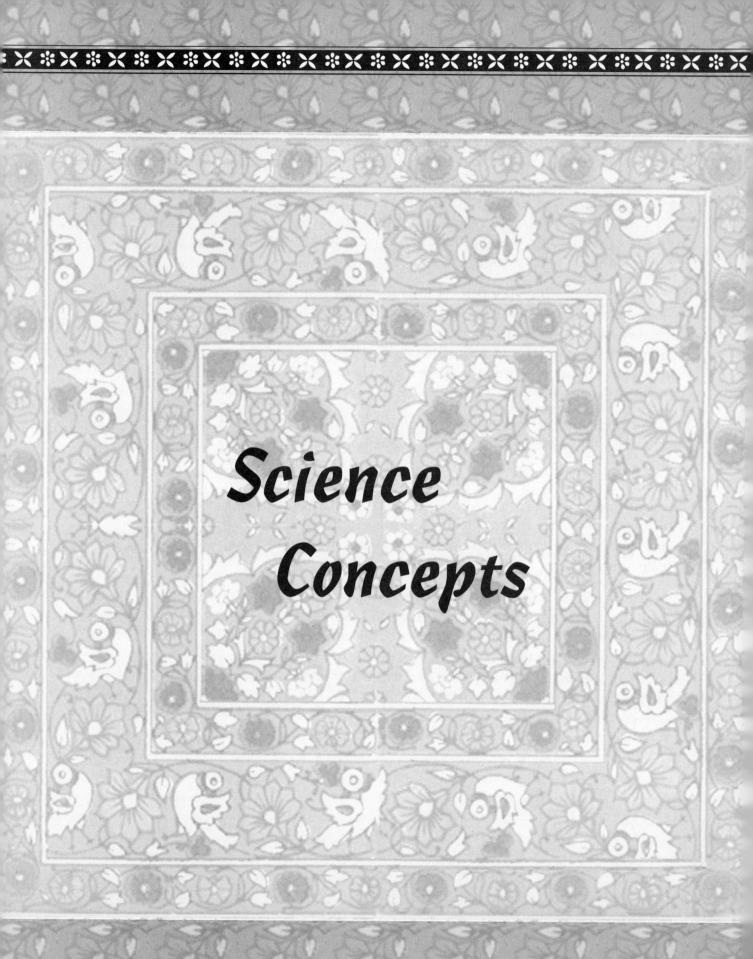

Science Concepts

UNIT 1

EARTH

EARTH

Rocks & Minerals

LITERATURE

Newton, P. *The Stonecutter.* New York: G. P. Putnam's Sons, 1990.

An Indian folk tale about a stonecutter's desire for ever-greater riches brings him a most surprising treasure.

Reasoner, C. *The Magic Amber.* Mahwah, New Jersey: Troll Associates, 1994.

The story tells of the mysterious power of Amber in a tale from Korea about an old farmer and his wife.

BACKGROUND INFORMATION

Rocks form on and beneath the Earth's surface. All rocks are made up of minerals. The minerals in some rocks are single elements such as gold or copper. But the minerals in most rocks are compounds, which are combinations of elements. Most minerals form crystals.

In volcanic Japan, rocks are everywhere. The Japanese rock garden is a high art form. Rock gardens are designed to look as if they are a natural part of a rocky hillside. A few large boulders usually look better than a number of small rocks. Many smaller plants usually fill spaces in cracks among rock faces. The main rocks from which rock gardens are constructed are sandstone and limestone.

Activity: Rock Gardens

Materials: (for each pair or small group)

- An assortment of small rocks
- Flat clay pots or sturdy paper plates
- Sand or pebbles

Divide the class into pairs or small groups. Have each pair choose a favorite rock and describe it. Have children make gardens inside flat clay pots or paper plates. Ask children to line the plates with pebbles or sand, and place their rock in an artistic spot on the plate. Help children decide what the rock symbolizes. Allow time for children to listen to each other's rock-garden stories.

Activity: **Sorting Rocks**

Materials: (for each pair of children)

- Variety of rocks
- Chart paper
- Marker

Ask students to pick a partner for this game. To play, each pair of students will need a variety of rocks. Instruct one student in each pair to sort some of their rocks into two groups, according to one property (color, texture, and so on). Can their partner tell which property was used to sort them? Try other single properties; encourage each partner to take turns choosing a property.

Next, students can play the I'm-Thinking-of-a-Rock game (also with a partner).Tell one student in each pair to place four or more rocks in a row. Encourage them to only think of just one rock and some of its properties. Can their partner pick out the "mystery" rock? The student doing the guessing must ask only questions that can be answered by *yes* or *no*.

After students have had a number of hands-on experiences with rocks, encourage them to discuss how they described their rocks. Explain to them that scientists usually find a way to keep track of the items they are studying. How well are students able to describe their collection of rocks? Can they make a chart that a partner can use to identify them? Encourage the students to make a chart of all properties they can observe about their rocks. Suggest to them they call their rocks *A, B,* and so on. They need to remember which rock is which. Allow different partners to use the chart to study the collection of rocks.

ETHNO SCIENCE FACT

The Kush people of Africa were experts in the art of working with silver and gold. They extracted and refined iron, using blast furnaces, as early as 250 B.C.

EARTH
Below the Surface

LITERATURE

Argueta, M. *Magic Dogs of the Volcanoes.* San Francisco: The Children's Book Press, 1990.

Magic dogs called cadejos live on the volcanoes of El Salvador. This Salvadoran folk tale tells of a time when the cadejos were hunted and had to call upon the help of the volcanoes.

Finsand, M. *The Town That Moved.* Minneapolis: Carolrhoda Books, Inc., 1983.

After cyclones blew over trees, iron ore was discovered in the holes they left behind. As a result, an entire town (full of people from many different countries) was moved for the purpose of mining the ore.

Lewis, T. *Hill of Fire.* New York: Harper & Row, 1971.

This is the true story of the eruption of a volcano in Mexico which occurred in 1943. A farmer was surprised when the ground opened up and a volcano started right in the middle of his cornfield. The farmer and the villagers of Paricutín witnessed a mountain grow. It grew 1,500 feet in eight months!

BACKGROUND INFORMATION

Earth is made up of three basic layers. The outermost layer is called the crust. Beneath that is a thick layer called the mantle. Occupying the central region is the core. The average thickness of the crust under the oceans is 3 miles, but under the continents the average thickness is 19 miles. The mantle has never been seen. All information about the mantle has come from measuring seismic waves, which are the vibrations caused by earthquakes. The mantle is about 1,800 miles thick. The core extends outward for about 2,160 miles. Obtaining information about the Earth's interior is so difficult that many ideas about its structure remain uncertain. The inner core, which has a radius of about 780 miles, is rigid, but the outer core surrounding it is almost liquid.

When a volcano erupts, hot molten rock and ashes are pushed out from the interior of the Earth through a hole

or crack in the surface. The molten rock pours out of the crack and flows across the Earth's surface, covering everything in its path. Most ashes blown out of the volcano settle in deep layers nearby, but some of the fine ash is blown out with such force that it goes into the upper atmosphere. Winds may carry it for hundreds of miles. When lava from a volcano solidifies, it is called igneous rock, which means rock formed by heat. Even though much of the Earth's crust is igneous rock, only a small part of the rock came from volcanoes.

Japan is built on fragile, volcanic islands. Japan consists of four major islands and hundreds of tiny volcanic islands. Honshu is the most populated. Earthquakes and volcanic action continually change and build the islands. Mt. Fuji is the most famous volcano. It is known for its beautiful cone.

Activity: A Volcano

Materials: (for the class)

- Glass bottle
- Play dough or papier mâché
- Baking soda
- Red vinegar
- Red food coloring (optional)

Safety: Be sure that children stand back after the baking soda and vinegar are mixed.

Children will enjoy making their own volcano. One method is to use a glass bottle as the spout of the volcano. Around the glass, build the cone with play dough or papier mâché. Combine baking soda and red vinegar at a 3:1 ratio, pour the mixture into the volcano top, watch Fuji erupt, and note the lava flow. (Add a few drops of red food coloring for extra excitement!) Children can compare their volcano with a video or film of an actual volcanic eruption. How are they the same? How are they different? What damage could be caused by a volcano? Where are other volcanoes located around the world? How often do they erupt? Which volcano is the tallest? The shortest? Which one erupts the most or the least?

The 1991 eruption of long dormant Mount Pinatubo was studied by Philippine volcanologist Raymundo Punongbayan. He also serves as the Director of the Philippine Institute of Volcanology and Seismology.

Activity: Candle Continents

Materials: (for the class)

- Wax candles
- Large metal pan
- Water
- Stove or hot plate

This activity will help children understand that the continents were formed when lighter molten rock floated upon heavier rock and hardened. First, guide children in carefully boiling several candles vigorously in a glass baking dish full of water. When the candles are nearly melted, tell the class that this is what the earth was like a long time ago. It was composed of several liquid substances all mixed together and very hot. Ask: "What do you think will happen when we allow the water and wax mixture to cool?" Accept guesses from the class and then allow the mixture to cool. After the mixture has cooled nearly to room temperature, ask these questions: "What do we see?" (The wax is floating on the water and is growing hard.) "If the water represents the hot, molten rocks of the earth's mantle, what does the wax represent?" (The crust.) Have the children draw a sketch of the earth as it was when it was a cooling molten ball.

Activity: The Earth's Crust

Materials: (for each child)

- Paper plate
- Slice of white bread
- Peanut butter
- Dark pumpernickel bread
- Raisins
- Brown bread
- Green mint jelly

Children can experience firsthand the layers of the Earth's crust by creating a special sandwich. Guide the children through the following steps. Before explaining to the children what each layer represents, give them the opportunity to come up with their own explanations.

1. Give each child a paper plate. What could this represent? (This empty plate represents *igneous bedrock*.)

2. Tell the children to pretend that there's a river flowing over the bedrock. Sand is being carried along in the water. The sand actually comes from rocks that are being broken down by the river. Over many years, the sand is pressed together to form sandstone. Instruct students to put down a slice of white bread. What would this represent? *(The sandstone.)*

3. Next, ask the students to pretend that, several years after the sandstone is formed, there is a flood. If a flood occurred, what do students think would happen to the sandstone? (Mud and rocks would be swept over the sandstone.) Students can spread peanut butter over the white bread to represent the mud and rocks. Encourage them to add several raisins for big rocks. This mud, rock, and boulder mixture becomes a *conglomerate*.

4. As time passes, the water carries small bits of rock called silt. Over many years, the layers of silt turns into shale rock. Students can place a slice of brown bread over their conglomerate to represent the shale.

5. Tell the children that this happened a long time ago. After the shale rock was formed, the Ice Age ended. Glaciers started to melt. When the glaciers melted, the oceans rose and covered the existing layers of rock. Throughout the years, creatures in the ocean died, and their shells and skeletons fell to the ocean floor. Over many years, this layer became *limestone*. Students can place a layer of green mint jelly on the brown bread to represent the limestone.

6. Finally, ask children to pretend that, for many years, it does not rain. Strong winds pick up particles of eroded rock. (Ask children if they have ever seen a "dust devil.") The particles swirl against a mountainside, and you get a layer of brown sand. Over many years, this layer becomes *brown*

sandstone. Students can finish their sandwiches with a slice of dark pumpernickel bread to represent the brown sandstone.

7. Next, the class can review what each part of the sandwich represents.

8. Students can have fun eating all their layers of the Earth's crust!

Activity: Layers of the Earth

Materials: (for each child or small group)

- Play dough: red, yellow, blue, green
- Fishing line or fine wire

After students understand the layers of the Earth's crust, they can do the following activity to show what is under the crust. This is a fun way for children to see for themselves the layers of the Earth.

Give students four different colors of play dough. Direct them to roll the red dough into a round ball. Next, have children make the yellow dough into a pancake. Then have them put the red ball inside the pancake and wrap it all up inside (now only the yellow shows). Do the same with the blue dough. Finally, the students can use the green to make the land formations and continents on top of the blue ball. When the globe is finished, ask the children to describe what they just made. Have them predict what the inside of their miniature Earth looks like. Ask them to figure out a way to open up their Earth and look inside. When they decide to cut it open, you can give them a small piece of fishing line (or thin wire) and show them how to use it to slice their globe in half. Children are always amazed to see their Earth after it is opened up!

Discussion: Construction in an Earthquake Area

Discuss with students the importance of using good building construction in an area that may be likely to experience an earthquake. Share pictures or videos of buildings before, during, and after earthquakes. Encourage students to think about the buildings in their area, such as their school, home, place of worship, and grocery store. Do they think that their school or home is built strong enough to survive an earthquake? Why or why not?

Background Information

Earthquake pressures react differently in different types of soil formation. There are several types of soil structures. The following activity will explore four of them: solid bedrock, soft soil, slopes that tend to slide, and muddy soils.

Activity: Earthquake-Resistant Construction

Materials: (for each small group)

- Vanilla wafers
- Bananas, sliced thin
- Pudding
- Pan (microwave-proof if using a microwave oven)
- Stove or microwave oven
- Layer cake (from conventional or microwave mix)
- Whipped cream
- Thick fudge or thick, solid brownies
- Blocks of flavored gelatin
- Chocolate wafers, crushed
- Green sprinkles
- Also see listings under Suggestions for Buildings.

Explain to the students that they will be making a different "edible" soil each day for four days. They will also be able to make buildings out of food to place on their soil types.

Suggestions for Buildings

- Building blocks: sugar cubes, soup bouillon cubes, cereals
- Building beams: straight stick pretzels, bread sticks
- Concrete foundations: vanilla wafers, other crackers
- Cement to connect building pieces: frosting, honey, or melted chocolate

Day One *Muddy soils:* Put lots of very thin pudding in the bottom of a pan. Then layer with small pieces of vanilla wafers and more pudding; and top with thinly sliced bananas.

Day Two *Sliding slopes:* Bake a layer cake. When it is still hot from the oven or microwave, put whipped cream between the layers.

Day Three *Solid bedrock:* Make thick fudge or thick, solid brownies.

Day Four *Soft soil:* Fold blocks of flavored gelatin into a large dish of whipped cream. Cover with crushed chocolate wafers and green sprinkles to give the appearance of solid soil.

Students can experiment with their buildings each day to compare how the soil behaves with a building and without a building. They can also compare how their buildings survive an earthquake on each of the different soil types. At the end of each day, students can eat their buildings and soil types. The teacher can discuss this activity with children by guiding them through questions such as these.

- Which type of soil was the best to build a safe house on? Why?
- If an earthquake struck, which soil would be the least safe for a building to be on? Why?
- How did you make your buildings stronger?
- Was it important to have a strong, secure foundation? How did you make one?
- If you had to live in a place that had solid bedrock or sliding slopes under you, which would be safer?
- What kinds of things could be built on muddy soils? Why?
- Could people make their sliding slopes more solid so that they would be safer during an earthquake? How could students change the cake and whipped cream to make it more solid?
- What could happen to the solid bedrock to make it less safe? What could they do to their brownies to make them less sturdy and strong?

LITERATURE

Baylor, B. *When Clay Sings.* New York: Atheneum, 1981.

The author describes what life may have been like during prehistoric times for Southwest Native Americans. Native Americans believed that a piece of clay represented a piece of someone's life and had its own small voice and sang in its own way.

Beatty, P. *Digging for China.* Englewood Cliffs, New Jersey: Silver Burdett & Ginn Inc., 1989.

During an archaeology dig, a simple jade bead is found and this leads to new discoveries about the past and the present in the lives of Peter and Martha.

Hoyt-Goldsmith, D. & L. Migdale. *Pueblo Storyteller.* New York: Holiday, 1991.

This story is about a young Cochiti Native American girl. She celebrates her family heritage through Cochiti pottery and storytelling. The book concludes with a Pueblo legend.

BACKGROUND INFORMATION

Clay is a layer of the Earth's crust. It is a substance that is easy to find for a variety of experiments and projects. Soil that has a lot of clay in it can be dug up, or clay can be purchased from an art-supply store. Discuss some possible meanings for symbols that are used in Native American stories. Talk about why the Native Americans would use red clay. Tell the students that the clay they will use for this activity is similar to clay that was used by Native Americans.

Activity: Medallion

Materials: (for each child)

- Clay
- Yarn
- Waxed paper
- Drinking straw
- Toothpick
- String
- Paints, brush, feathers (optional)

EARTH

Exploring the Past

ETHNO SCIENCE FACT

Clay-pot batteries were made in Persia c. 250 B.C. Each clay pot battery contained a vinegar-filled copper tube with an iron or bronze rod at its center and had an output of 0.5–2.0 volts.

Give each student a lump of clay, some waxed paper, a toothpick, and some yarn. Have students shape their clay into a medallion. Have them use their toothpicks to scratch designs in their clay. Have students use a straw to put a hole in the top center of the medallion. This will give the student a place to string the yarn so the medallion can be worn around the neck. Allow the clay to dry overnight. After it is dry, students may wish to paint their designs. They may also attach feathers or string to the medallion.

BACKGROUND INFORMATION

The science of fossils is called *paleontology.* The science of extinct animals is *paleozoology.* The science of extinct plants is *paleobotany.*

By studying fossils, scientists have been able to piece together some of the important pages in the history of the Earth and its people. Fossils show that the great coal and chalk beds of the world were formed from the remains of living things. Millions of years ago tiny animals were making shells that became the limestone of today.

Activity: Fossils

Materials: (for the teacher)

- Plaster of Paris
- Water

Materials: (for each child)

- Waxed drinking cup or milk carton with the top cut off
- Small objects (seashell, button, key)
- Petroleum jelly

This activity will help children understand how scientists can infer many things from examining fossils.

Mix water with plaster of Paris to form a paste. Pour the plaster into waxed containers to a depth of about one inch and distribute them to groups of children. Have the children cover the surface of a seashell, button, or key with

ETHNO SCIENCE FACT

Hispanic American Physicist Luis W. Alvarez (b. 1911) won the 1968 Nobel Prize for Physics. In 1980, working with his son, geologist Walter Alvarez, he found evidence that suggests that the mass extinction of dinosaurs was caused by the collision of a meteor or comet with Earth.

petroleum jelly, and push it gently into the plaster of Paris. Allow the plaster to dry, and remove the object carefully. A mold of the object will be left in the plaster cast.

If the students were paleontologists, what would they be able to conclude from their plaster "fossil"? What would a key tell them? (Students might respond with ideas on locks, dwellings, need for security, and so on.) What would a button tell them? (People needed buttons for clothing.) What clue would the seashell give them? (A body of water once was at this location.)

Activity: Time Capsule

Materials: (for the class)

- Large, clean trash can
- Discarded school work
- Tape measure

Tell students that they are going to create a miniature history of their classroom for a period of one week. After seven days, they will be able to excavate their site to find out clues about their week. During the week, ask students to deposit their papers into the special can. Most of the paper can be the regular waste that normally can be found in class. Some of the papers should include the date. Make plans to put a special note or drawing in the can occasionally throughout the week. Students may have to push the paper down during the week.

At excavation time, students can carefully go through the trash, layer by layer. They should use a tape measure to record the depth at which papers and other special artifacts are found. Where are the newest layers? The oldest? How are paper layers like layers of rock in the Earth? If an undated paper is found near a dated one, can you guess the age of the undated paper? Why might different dates be near one another? What forces could have changed the papers? Could squishing, stomping, stirring, or accidental spills change the natural arrangement of the trash? How would this compare with the layers of the Earth and what we can find out about our past?

EAR|H

Protecting Our Future

George, J. *The Talking Earth.* New York: HarperCollins, 1983.

In this story, Billie Wind lives with her Seminole tribe. She goes out into the Everglades alone, to stay until she can believe and no longer doubt Seminole legends about talking animals and earth spirits.

Holcroft, A. *Chen Li and the River Spirit.* London: Hodder and Stoughton, 1991.

A man is undeterred by hardship to reforest the Valley of Leaping Water. The story involves five recurring Chinese characters with a focus on self-sacrifice, endurance, and environmental issues.

Baker, J. *Window.* New York: Greenwillow, 1991.

As a young boy grows to manhood in Australia, the scene outside his window changes: housing gradually replaces the forest lands.

Chief Seattle. *Brother Eagle, Sister Sky: A Message from Chief Seattle.* New York: Dial, 1991.

This is an adaptation of a message attributed to Chief Seattle of the Suquamish and Duwamish tribes. The Chief encourages everyone to care for and preserve our environment.

Fife, D. *The Empty Lot.* Boston: Sierra Club, Little Brown, 1991.

This story tells about a small patch of land and the creatures who call it home.

George, J. *Who Really Killed Cock Robin? An Ecological Mystery.* New York: HarperCollins, 1991.

Through the involvement of many environmental issues, a mystery is solved.

BACKGROUND INFORMATION

The reasonable use of Earth's natural resources—water, soil, wildlife, forests, and minerals—is a major goal of conservation. An effective conservation program results in a steady supply of native plants, animals, and mineral resources. The prevention of environmental pollution, including toxic chemicals and radioactive wastes, is another concern of conservation. People concerned with conservation seek to prevent the waste of natural resources, to maintain a high-quality environment, and to preserve the natural heritage for future generations.

Natural resources are sometimes classified as renewable or nonrenewable. Forests, grasslands, wildlife, and soil are examples of renewable resources. Such resources as coal, petroleum, and iron ore are nonrenewable.

Activity: Conservation

Materials: (for each group)

• Counters

This activity will introduce the concept of conservation as a survival skill for people, and ultimately, Earth. Begin the lesson by discussing two things: needs and wants. Needs are things people must have to live, while wants are things people would like to have. Students need water and food to survive. They may want toys, for example, but they would not die if they didn't have any. The students can be instructed that, for this activity, they will each be responsible for collecting and finding their own food for survival.

Divide the students into groups of ten, and explain that the people in each group will compete for food to survive. The counters used in this activity will represent food. Explain that the goal for each person is to get five counters in order to have enough food to eat and stay

healthy. Explain that the number of counters left in the center pile at the end of the first game will be doubled in the next round. (Students will probably think of themselves only at this point and not work cooperatively.)

Place 15 counters on the table, and tell the children that, when you say "go," they can take the counters. They are not allowed to talk during the activity.

Discuss what happened in the groups. Were the food counters fairly shared? Did everyone get enough food counters? Were there enough food counters left to ensure a supply of food for the next game? What could students do more efficiently next time? Explain that, if students take only what they need, they are conserving the resource—practicing conservation.

Define *conservation* as people taking only what they need of the different resources. Explain that they must also do something to make sure that the resource will be usable for the next years.

Go around and replenish all the food stores. Make sure every group has 15 food counters. Give the students five minutes to discuss how they should distribute the food counters in their group. (Remind them that counters left after each round *double*.) Say "go," and let them take the counters.

After students finish for the second time discuss the results. Was it important to work together? Was the resource renewable? Could they go out and get more counters from another classroom? Did they have to take care of the resource? What did they have to do to make sure that everyone got enough of the resource?

Ask each child to discuss examples of ways people apply conservation today. Each child can work with friends and family members to design a plan to practice conservation at school and at home.

BACKGROUND INFORMATION

In Australia, there have been many dangers to the environment including the hunt for animals. Kangaroos and wallabies (smaller relatives of the kangaroo) were slaughtered for pet food and for their fur, or because they allegedly posed a threat to the grazing lands of sheep and cattle. A public outcry has slowed the pace of the killings. At one time, the koala was in danger of extinction, but it now enjoys legal protection. The platypus was in danger of being exterminated by fur hunters but is now protected by law.

Discussion: Australia

Children can discuss the type of environment one would see in Australia. How would the scene outside their own window be different from the one in Australia? Important questions can be raised with the children: Do we need to protect all land areas? Why or why not? Are there alternatives to destroying forests in order to house people? What type of cooperation between the needs of people and the benefits of saving local land and trees is possible today?

BACKGROUND INFORMATION

At the beginning of the twentieth century, most solid waste was disposed of by dumping it onto vacant land near where it was generated. Concern over health hazards led to the development of sanitary landfills. Here the refuse is compacted to about one tenth of its original volume. It is then disinfected and put into cells that are covered daily with earth.

Experts have determined that a third of the landfills in the United States will reach their capacity by the mid-1990s. The introduction of new landfills, however, has met with significant opposition from environmentalists and from residents around proposed sites. There is, for

ETHNO SCIENCE FACT

Aboriginal Australians developed sophisticated ecological knowledge and used controlled fires to manage land resources. Aboriginal elders are now consulted about land management in Australian national parks.

instance, evidence that biodegradable materials dumped in landfills do not significantly decompose even after several decades.

Activity: Living Organisms

Materials: (for each group)

- Craft sticks
- Thermometer
- String
- Hand lens
- Meter stick
- Paper and pencil

Break the class up into groups of three or four, and supply each group with materials. Have each group mark off a meter-square section of ground outside. Encourage students to select a variety of locations.

Have students list all the different kinds of plants and animals in their study area. If they wish, they can further subdivide the square into quarters or eighths to make their observations more precise. Have students record the temperature at different locations in the plot. To motivate students, you might make this a contest to see which group can find the most living organisms in its square.

Safety: Have students wash their hands after handling soil.

As a whole group, discuss the findings. List all the living organisms on the board, and try to get class members to explain why certain locations have more organisms than others. Possible explanations include temperature, shade, water, and the influence of humans.

Try this activity at a different time of the day, and see what effect this has on the observations. Also try the same activity at a different time of the year, or take a representative square and follow it systematically during the school year. Discuss different ways people can change the ecology of an area. Have students try to identify both good and bad aspects of these changes.

Activity: Decomposition

Materials: (for the class)

- Banana peel
- Sheet of notebook paper
- Shovel

Children may not have an idea of the impact they can have on the environment each time they litter. Ask the children to predict how long the following items would take to decompose. Have the children make a chart showing their predictions and then the actual facts next to each one. Before finding out the actual facts, the children may wish to conduct a mini-experiment. Help the children bury a banana peel and a piece of notebook paper in a hole
dug in the schoolyard. Have them check after one week. Give them the opportunity to adjust their original predictions for the following list of products. After their mini-experiment, they may gain a new insight into how long it takes for something to actually decompose.

Product	Prediction	Fact
Aluminum can	_____	_____
Banana peel	_____	_____
Cardboard milk carton	_____	_____
Car tire	_____	_____
Comic book	_____	_____
Cotton diaper	_____	_____
Glass bottle	_____	_____
Notebook paper	_____	_____
Plastic sandwich bag	_____	_____
Plastic six-pack ring	_____	_____
Polystyrene foam cup	_____	_____
Steel can	_____	_____
Toothbrush	_____	_____

Facts for Students

- A banana peel takes 2 months; notebook paper takes 3 months; and a cotton diaper takes 4 months to decompose.

- It takes 6 months for a comic book to decompose.

- Cardboard milk cartons take 5 years to decompose.

- A steel can takes 100 years to decompose. Aluminum cans take 350 years to decompose.

- A toothbrush and a plastic sandwich bag both will decompose after 400 years.

- A plastic six-pack ring will take 450 years to decompose.

- Some items may never decompose, such as a polystyrene foam cup, a car tire, or a glass bottle.

Source: Hadingham, Janet & Evan. *Garbage! Where It Comes From, Where It Goes.* New York: Simon and Schuster, 1990.

UNIT 2

OCEANS

Water

LITERATURE

Lessac, F. *My Little Island.* New York: Harper & Row Publishers, 1984.

A young boy and his best friend, Lucca, return to visit the little Caribbean island where he was born.

Taylor, T. *The Cay.* New York: Doubleday, 1969.

Phillip is stranded on a raft off a tiny island in St. Anna's Channel and learns to survive through many difficult situations.

Activity: Ocean Water

Materials: (for the whole class)

- Salt
- Water
- Measuring teaspoon
- Two large bowls
- Measuring cup

Materials: (for each child)

- Water
- Salt
- Bowl
- Food coloring
- Measuring cup
- Construction paper
- Brushes

Children can duplicate a method scientists used to first discover that there was salt in the ocean. First, show the children how to make ocean water by mixing four teaspoons of salt with four cups of water. Next, ask the children to pour the four cups of ocean water into a big bowl. In another bowl, have the children pour four cups of plain water (without added salt) to represent fresh water. Place both of the bowls in a warm, dry place—perhaps near a window sill. Allow the water to evaporate. This will usually take about two days. Discuss with the children the differences between the two water samples.

Another fun activity to reinforce this concept is the creation of evaporation pictures. Mix one cup of water, 1/2 cup of salt, and a few drops of food coloring in a cup. Instruct the children to use brushes to paint this mixture onto construction paper. After the water dries, the children will still see the color and salt on the paper in a pretty, sparkling image.

Activity: Floating on Water

Materials: (for the whole class)

- Two identical bowls, labeled *A* and *B*
- Warm water
- Salt
- Eggs
- Measuring teaspoon
- Large spoon

Children can explore the unique properties that salt water has. They can answer the question: Would it be easier for them to float in ocean water or in fresh water? Guide the children through the following experiment.

1. Put the same amount of warm water (about 8 oz.) into two identical bowls.
2. Dissolve 12 teaspoons of salt in bowl B. It will be necessary to stir vigorously.
3. Carefully place an egg in bowl A and an egg in bowl B.
4. What can students observe?
5. What can they conclude?
6. What does this experiment prove about floating on water? What does this experiment tell about ships in the ocean?

Activity: Water Density

Materials: (for the whole class)

- Five glasses
- Cold salt water
- Cold fresh water
- Hot salt water
- Hot fresh water
- Four different food colorings
- Spoon
- Ice (optional)

Polynesians built large, voyaging canoes. By the year 1000, they had explored and settled a 39-million square-kilometer area bounded by New Zealand, Hawaii, and Easter Island. They navigated thousands of miles of open sea, using their knowledge of astronomy, ocean currents, and wave patterns.

Pour cold salt water into one glass, cold fresh water in the second, hot salt water in the third, and hot fresh water in the fourth. Add a few drops of a different food coloring to each glass and stir. (The food coloring makes it easier to tell the liquids apart. It doesn't affect the density.) In another glass, carefully pour in a layer of each liquid, going from the most dense to the least dense: cold salt water on the bottom; cold fresh water next; then hot salt water; and, finally, hot fresh water. Be careful not to mix the layers as you pour them into the glass. Tilt the glass slightly and run a new liquid along the side of the glass as you add a layer. Experiment with different water temperatures and different amounts of salt. Make sure there are real differences in the temperatures of the water samples. If it takes too long to do the experiment, begin again by reheating the water or adding ice to water that may not be cold enough. Ask students to discuss what they observe.

LITERATURE

Siy, A. *The Eeyou: People of Eastern James Bay.* New York: Dillon Press, Inc., 1993.

This is the story of how the introduction of a hydroelectric plant affected the balance of the ecosystem. The Eeyou are also known as the Cree Indians.

BACKGROUND INFORMATION

Water gives up some of its potential energy when it flows from a higher level to a lower level. The potential energy changes to *kinetic energy* (energy of motion) as the water falls. The moving water can be made to turn a bladed wheel so that the kinetic energy is transformed into mechanical energy. The shaft of the bladed wheel is usually attached to gears, levers, and different types of machines. In the past, mechanical energy from water wheels was used to grind grain and saw timber. Today, moving water is used to generate electricity.

Activity: Water Wheel

Materials: (for each group)

- Drinking straws
- Empty spools
- String or twine
- Rubber bands of different sizes
- Paper clips
- Two big pans
- Small paper or plastic cups (2–4 oz. size)
- Tongue depressors or craft sticks
- Glue
- Tape
- Paper and pencil

Children can be challenged to make a water wheel that can actually be used to transport a small amount of water. Divide the children into groups, and give them materials.

Encourage children to discuss ways in which their group can make a simple machine that will pick up water from one pan, carry it a short distance, and dump it into another pan. They should draw their invention first on paper before actually constructing it.

OCEANS

Water As Energy

ETHNO SCIENCE FACT

The Maori people of New Zealand developed cooking methods that used natural energy. They built oven boxes to use over natural steam vents and used hot springs for boiling foods.

After construction is finished, allow each group to demonstrate their water wheel to the class and explain how they made it. They should also discuss possible changes they might make to their design, if they wish to make it more efficient.

Water Wheel

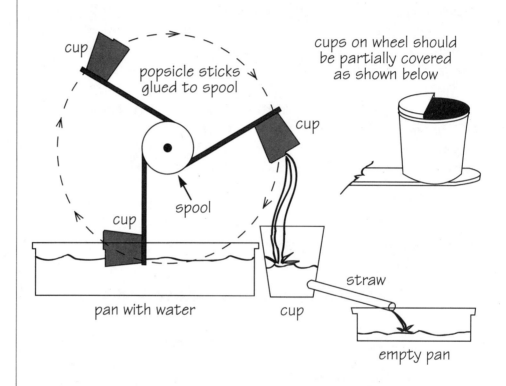

cup

popsicle sticks glued to spool

cup

cups on wheel should be partially covered as shown below

spool

cup

pan with water

cup

straw

empty pan

LITERATURE

Lewin, H. and L. Kopper. *A Shell on the Beach.* London: Hamish Hamilton, 1989.
A child is disappointed when she discovers a dirty and polluted beach.

BACKGROUND INFORMATION

Water has always been used to carry away unwanted refuse. Rivers, streams, canals, lakes, and oceans are filled with many kinds of pollution. Waste materials that eventually decompose are called biodegradable. However, more serious pollutants such as metals, plastics, and some chlorinated hydrocarbons remain in the water and become poisonous. As water becomes filled with any form of contamination, life within the water starts to suffer. Factories, too, sometimes dump harmful wastes into water. Agricultural runoff containing dangerous pesticides can also be a source of pollution.

Most cities have water treatment plants to clean their drinking water. As the water filters through, polluting materials are left behind.

Activity: **Clean Water**

Materials: (for each small group)

- Empty milk carton
- Nail
- Cotton
- Clean sand
- Crushed charcoal briquette (without starter fluid added)
- Small bag
- Rock
- Three small glass jars
- Clean tap water
- Soil
- Food coloring

Students can find out about the difficulty of purifying water in the following activity. Ask children to think of a way to clean polluted water by filtering. After discussing their answers, explain to them that they are going to try one way and then, perhaps, try out their own methods. Guide the students through the following steps.

1. With a nail, punch some holes in the bottom of a milk carton.

2. Spread some cotton inside on the bottom of the carton. Add clean sand.

3. Put a crushed charcoal briquette on top of the sand. (To crush charcoal, put a briquette into a small bag and pound it.) Then add another layer of sand.

4. Place the milk-carton filter on top of the glass jar.

5. Pour some clean tap water into the filter.

6. Prepare a jar of soil water. Put a handful of soil into a jar of water and mix. Let the water settle for half an hour.

7. Place the filter on an empty glass jar. Pour some water from the top of the soil-water jar into the filter. Watch the filtered water trickle into the jar.

Guide a student discussion after children see the result of this experiment. The following questions can serve as a guide for the discussion.

- How clean is the filtered water compared with the soil water?

- How clean would the water get with fewer filtering materials?

- Will this filter remove ink or food coloring?

- Does the order in which we have the filter materials matter?

- How could you improve the filter?

BACKGROUND INFORMATION

Oil can kill animals and plants that live in the water. If the oil sinks to the bottom of a body of water or covers beaches, it does not allow animals like oysters and clams to reproduce; if the animals are able to reproduce, the offspring are usually affected. Birds that get covered in oil are unable to fly and their feathers lose the ability to keep the birds warm. Oil in water isn't easy to clean up. Some oil spill clean-up methods can be as damaging to the environment as the oil itself.

Activity: Oil Spill

Materials: (for each small group)

- Water
- Cooking oil colored with food coloring
- Eyedropper
- Two shallow 9" × 13" pans
- Feather
- Cotton balls
- Fabric scraps
- Paper towels
- Dishwashing liquid

Ahead of time: *Add a few drops of food coloring to the cooking oil.*

To give children the opportunity to create and experiment with their own "oil spill," guide them through the following steps.

1. Fill a pan with water.

2. Create an "oil spill" in the water by adding five to ten drops of oil. Does the oil mix with the water?

3. Create waves on the "ocean" in the pan by blowing on the water or moving it gently. What happens to the oil? Why would it be important to clean up an oil spill quickly?

4. Dip a feather into the oil spill. What happens? How would oily feathers affect a bird?

5. Which material—cotton balls, fabric, or paper towels—cleans up the spill best? Test each material. Make new spills as needed. How much oil is cleaned up by each material? How quickly can you clean up the spill? What problems do you have? What happens to the oil as time goes on? How difficult would it be to clean up the spill, if there were a terrible storm?

6. Create an oil spill (five to ten drops of oil) in another pan filled with water. Add five drops of dishwashing liquid. What happens to the oil? Where would the oil go in a real ocean? How clean is the water now that it has dishwashing liquid in it? What's worse— oil or the dishwashing liquid?

OCEANS

Whales

LITERATURE

Roy, R. *A Thousand Pails of Water.* New York: Random House, Inc., 1978.

A young boy is determined to save a stranded whale in a whaling village (in Japan), where almost everyone makes a living by hunting whales. The entire village becomes inspired to help the boy save the beached whale.

Ryder, J. *Winter Whale.* New York: Morrow, 1991.

A humpback whale journeys to warm tropical waters for winter and returns to cold water for the summer.

BACKGROUND INFORMATION

Whales live in all the open seas of the world. The present-day abundance of some species has been greatly influenced by the whaling industry. The blue whale was almost completely exterminated in the early 1900s.

The skin of whales is usually black, gray, black and white, or all white. Some, such as the blue whale, have skin that is bluish-gray. The surface of the skin is smooth, but like other mammals, whales have hair. Whales have lungs, not gills, so they must come to the surface of the ocean to breathe.

Whales are able to swim up to 35 miles per hour. Some whales are social, traveling in groups called schools, herds, or pods. A mother whale helps a newborn calf remain at the surface to breathe. Like dolphins and porpoises, some whales can be playful. Whales sometimes swim ashore and become stranded on a beach. When whales are washed ashore, they are helpless. Without the support of water they cannot move, and their lungs may be crushed by the weight of their body.

Whales have keenly-developed senses of sight and hearing. Whales are presumed to be color-blind. Hearing is a well-developed sense in whales.

Whales produce low-pitched signals, such as barks, whistles, screams, moans, and other sounds that are brief clicks of high intensity. These sounds are used for purposes of echolocation. The sounds are used for finding their way through the sea, and for locating each other and their prey. Because each whale pod has its own pattern of sounds, scientists believe the noises are a means of communication.

Activity: Lengths of Whales

Materials: (for each group)

- Paper
- Crayons or markers to match yarn colors
- Yarn, rolls in different colors
- Tape measure
- Tape or staples
- Science books or encyclopedia
- Graph paper

In this activity, students will compare lengths of three different whales. Divide your class into three groups and assign a whale to each group. Have students use science books or an encyclopedia to find the length of the whale assigned to their group. Then give a piece of paper to each group. Assist students as needed to follow these directions.

1. Have students write the name of their whale on both sides of the paper, large enough to be read from a distance. Then have them decorate the paper.

2. Give a different color roll of yarn to each group. Have students use a tape measure to measure out a length of yarn equal to the length of the whale they are representing.

3. Take the class outside; and have each group spread its length of yarn out in a straight line, parallel to those of the other groups. One end of each yarn should be even with the others.

4. Attach the pieces of paper with the names to each of the aligned ends of the yarn.

5. Compare the sizes of the whales, and discuss any questions or observations the students make.

6. Take the class back inside. Tape or staple each of the lengths of yarn around the room on the wall, like a bar graph with the beginning ends (the ends with the names attached) right inside the door.

7. Have the students make bar graphs using the same colors as the color of yarn used for each whale. Ask students to make comparisons and draw conclusions based on their graphs.

8. Repeat steps 1–7 with people and objects, such as a few students, the teacher, a car, a desk. This will allow students to compare things they see every day to the enormous size of a whale.

Activity: **Echolocation**

Materials: (for each group)

- Stickers or T-shirts, a different color for each group
- Noisemakers (rulers, marbles in a can, small bells, for example)
- Blindfolds

Safety: *Ask helpers from upper grades or, perhaps, parents to monitor the children as they walk around blindfolded.*

Students can experience how sound may be used to locate the position of a friend in the following experiment. Divide the class into three groups. Each group represents a whale pod. Identify each pod by having its members wear stickers (or T-shirts) of the same color.

1. Have each pod adopt its own call sound. For example, students might choose to tap rulers, rattle marbles in a can, or ring small bells. Make sure that one sound doesn't overpower any other sound.

2. Ask the class to assemble in a large open area, such as the playground. Have everyone move around— mixed up, not in any special order. Then have each child find a place to stand.

3. Blindfold all the students.

4. Silently lead one member (a leader whale) from each pod to a separate spot in the room.

5. Have the leader whales each remain in place and continuously sound the call of his or her pod.

6. Let all pod members set out to locate their leader, each repeating the pod's distinctive call throughout the search. Emphasize that the students should only communicate through their calls, not with their voices.

Students should continue the search until all members of the same pod are together. When almost all of the children have found their pods, the students can remove the blindfolds. Together, discuss what they have learned about whales and about humans from this experience.

LITERATURE

Ai-Ling, L. *Yeh-Shen: A Cinderella Story from China.* New York: Philomel Books, 1982.

A young girl overcomes the cruelty of a stepmother with the help of a magic fish.

Joseph, L. *Jasmine's Parlour Day.* New York: Lothrop, Lee & Shephard Books, 1994.

The story of island life in Trinidad and the importance of fish.

BACKGROUND INFORMATION

Many animals that live in water are called fish. A fish is a cold-blooded animal that has a backbone, lives in water, and breathes by means of gills. It normally has two pairs of fins in place of arms and legs, as well as several other fins. Many fish are covered with scales.

Activity: Boo, Fish!

Materials: (for the teacher)

- Flashlight

Materials: (for each group)

- Fish (guppies or goldfish) in a bowl with water
- Flashlight
- Marbles
- Fish food
- Paper and pencil

Fish, like people and other animals, respond to stimuli. Children can explore this concept in the following activity.

Stand in front of the darkened classroom. Shine the flashlight at several children, and ask: "Why did you look away from the light?" Point out that the children are responding to a stimulus. The light is the stimulus.

Then tell the children to put their heads on their desks. Tell them that, when they hear music, they

should lift their heads. Hum a few bars of a simple melody. Ask: "Why did you raise your heads? What was the stimulus? Will other, more simple, animals respond to a stimulus? How could we find out?"

Divide the children into groups of five or six. Provide each group with materials. Tell the children to observe how the fish respond to the stimuli of tapping gently on the bowl close to the fish, shining the flashlight directly on the fish, dropping a marble close to the fish, and putting fish food in the bowl. Have each group record its observations.

After each group has completed the experiment, discuss how the fish responded to stimuli. In each case, ask: "What was the stimulus? How did the fish respond?"

Activity: **Fish Prints**

Materials: (for each group)

- Frozen fish
- Newsprint
- Nontoxic paint— black, blue, red
- Brush
- Paper
- Marker

In Japan, fish are very important to the people. Japanese art often involves fish as a subject. Students can learn to make fish prints by following these steps.

1. Place a frozen fish on newsprint. Paint a layer of black, blue, or red paint on it. Then lay a piece of paper over it. Lightly press down without moving the paper; then peel off the paper.

2. Make sure that the gills and scales show well on the paper. If not, paint another thin layer of paint on the fish and repeat the process.

3. Draw and paint in the eye.

Marine Life

LITERATURE

Binch, C. *Gregory Cool*. New York: Dial, 1994.

The story is about an adventure on Tobago Island. It involves life on the beach and the excitement of sharks.

O'Dell, S. *The Black Pearl*. Boston: Houghton Mifflin Company, 1967.

Ramon Salazar lives in La Paz, Mexico, where his family makes its living pearling the waters of Baja, California. He has grown up hearing legends about the great Black Pearl.

Sperry, A. "Ghost of the Lagoon." *Fast As the Wind*. Boston: Houghton Mifflin, 1993.

Mako lives on the island of Bora Bora in the South Pacific. His expeditions into the sea involve many creatures.

Yep, L. *Sea Glass*. New York: Harper & Row, 1979.

Uncle Quail and his nephew explore the wonders beneath the sea's surface: abalones, barnacles, mussels, starfish, crabs, and sea urchins.

BACKGROUND INFORMATION

The oceans and seas are full of life. There are sea creatures, such as dolphins, eels, sharks, abalones, sardines, squid, octopus, lobster, sea urchin, tuna, whelk, jellyfish, sponges, oysters, coral, barnacles, mussels, clam, crabs, and sea anemones. There are plants that grow under the surface of the water: seaweed, algae, kelp, sea lettuce, sargassum, rockweed, lichen, fungi, and sea sandwort. Birds and other animals can be found near the ocean: seals, walruses, sea otters, pelicans, gulls, penguins, and puffins.

Activity: Umbrella Jellyfish

Materials: (for each child)

- Umbrella (brought from home)
- Crepe paper
- Tape
- Recording of soft, slow music
- Tape, record, or CD player

Explain that, in the water, a jellyfish looks like a fringed umbrella. Each child should tape crepe-paper streamers around his or her open umbrella to simulate jellyfish. Play a recording of slow and soft music. Encourage students to move the umbrella like a jellyfish.

Activity: Ocean Mural

Materials: (for the whole class)

- Butcher paper
- Paint, colored chalk, or crayons
- Construction paper
- Fabric scraps
- Scissors
- Glue
- Masking tape
- Old magazines (*National Geographic,* for example)
- Other craft supplies

Students can make a large ocean mural by following these directions.

1. Attach the butcher paper along one wall.

2. Paint the background like the ocean: light blue on top, progressing to dark blue on the bottom.

3. As the students learn about various marine life, they can make samples and place them on the mural. Students can also use florescent paint, so that various parts of the mural can glow in the dark.

4. Attach strips of blue cellophane above the cooling vent in the classroom. (An adult should do this.) When the air is blowing, the cellophane will simulate seaweed moving in the water.

5. Invite students and parents to visit the classroom. Each visitor can be asked to make or bring something to add to the mural. The mural can eventually be expanded to cover all the wall space in the classroom.

6. As guests tour the class, play soft instrumental music in the background.

Beaches and Shells

LITERATURE

Fuja, A. *Fourteen Hundred Cowries and Other African Tales.* New York: Lothrop, 1971.

Unusual stories recorded many years ago by a Yoruba scholar.

Gissing, V. *Joshua and the Big Wave.* E. Sussex, England: Macdonald Young Books, Ltd., 1989.

This is a folk tale from the Caribbean. It describes the story of Joshua and his concern to warn his family and the villagers of a big wave that is coming. As part of the plot, shells are collected for ornamental purposes.

Yep, L. *The Shell Woman and the King: A Chinese Folktale.* New York: Dial, 1993.

Good Wu marries a woman who can change herself into a shell.

BACKGROUND INFORMATION

Long ago, Native Americans used beads made from shells for decorating clothing and making jewelry. These shells were highly coveted, and often the settlers would use them to trade for furs and other supplies. In fact, at one time these shells were considered legal tender among the colonies. But it was very hard to cut, shape, and smooth the sea shells to just the right shape. Native Americans found commercial beads, brought by the settlers, a lot easier to use; and many stopped using the seashells.

Shells are like stone forts that animals build around themselves for protection. Shells are composed of substances secreted by the glands of the mollusks. They consist largely of the basic ingredient that is found in limestone, chalk, and marble. As a mollusk grows, so does its shell. The lines of growth are usually clearly marked by the ridges that run parallel to the outer edge of the shell. The outside of the shell may be a variety of colors, but usually has a pattern combining several tints, or shades. The color inside is usually paler and more delicate than it is outside the shell. Shells of the tropics are usually more

vividly colored than those found in cooler zones. Nearly all shells fall into one of two groups—univalves (with one-piece shells) and bivalves (with two-piece shells). The largest of the shells is the giant clam of the Indian and Pacific oceans, which grows to be from two to three feet in diameter and can sometimes weigh four hundred pounds.

Among many primitive peoples, shells were used for money. The most widely-used shells for this purpose were certain kinds of cowries, or Venus's shells. The ringed cowrie is still the usual currency in a few remote Indian and Pacific islands. Some tribes in the interior of Africa use strings of the money cowrie.

Activity: Bead Art

Materials: (for each group)

- Commercial beads or shells

- String or beading wire

- Ditali (pasta), liquid food coloring, container with lid, paper towels (optional)

- Plastic canvas, needle, thread (optional)

Ahead of time: *If your students are using ditali, place the pasta in a container with a few drops of liquid food coloring. With the container tightly covered, shake vigorously. Set the pasta on paper towels to dry.*

Let the students use the materials to bead necklaces, bracelets, or other items. Some students might choose to sew them through plastic canvas to make colorful designs, and then frame them. Older children could bring articles of clothing to decorate with the beads or shells by sewing them on with needle and thread.

Activity: Shell Money

Materials: (for the whole class)

- Large number of cowrie shells

- Buttons, stickers, or other counters (optional)

Tell the students that they are going to create a new place to live. In this place, there is no money as we know it. This place is on an island. What do they think they could use as money? What objects could be used? (Shells would be a good idea.) Explain that some tribes in Africa use shells today as a form of money. Allow the children to set up their economic system with the cowries (or other counters). Ask them to explain their system and demonstrate how it operates.

Ask students to explain why there would be so many shells around an island. Ask: "What would you do with the animals that live inside the shells? If the shells were already empty, where did the animal inside go? How do shells protect animals? Why don't larger animals, or even humans, have shells? How do we protect ourselves?"

UNIT 3

Weather

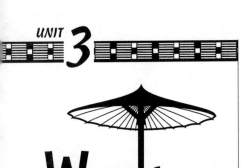

Weather

Rain

LITERATURE

Aardema, V. *Bringing the Rain to Kapiti Plain.*
New York: Dial Books for Young Readers, 1981.

This is a story about the rain, Ki-pat, and Ki-pat's herd of cows in Africa.

Bonnici, P. *The First Rains.* London: Mantra Publishing, 1984.

This is the story of Arjuna and preparations for the rainy season in India. The book includes information on climate, culture, and changing weather conditions.

Cruz, M. *Yagua Days.* New York: Dial, 1987.

Adan, a Puerto Rican child born in New York, thinks that rainy days are boring. He discovers what children in Puerto Rico do on rainy days. When the grass is slick with rain, he uses a yagua (a large palm leaf) to slide down the grassy hills and into the river.

Wisniewski, D. *Rain Player.* New York: Lothrop, 1992.

This story of rain is a tale from Mayan culture.

BACKGROUND INFORMATION

Native Americans have special ceremonies to pray for rain. The rainmaker has the responsibility for forecasting the weather. He uses the direction of the winds, the clouds, or the humidity and atmospheric pressure to make his decisions. [Driver, 1992]

Discussion: *Bringing the Rain to Kapiti Plain*

Materials: (for the teacher)

- Recording of weather and nature sounds
- Tape recorder, or CD player

During the reading of *Bringing the Rain to Kapiti Plain*, play a nature tape of various sounds. Choose one that has a variety of weather sounds. Play the rain sounds at the appropriate point during the story. After the story is read, discuss with the children the following questions: Do you

think clouds really break to spill out the rain? Do you think Ki-pat could make it rain with an arrow?

Activity: **Falling Rain**

Materials: (for the teacher)

- Measuring cup
- Water
- Teakettle
- Ice cubes
- Saucepan
- Stove or hot plate

Tell the students that they are going to observe an experiment that will show how rain is made.

1. Bring two cups of water in a teakettle to a boiling point so that the steam is rising from the spout.

2. Put ice cubes in a saucepan. Hold the saucepan over the spout of the teakettle so that the steam from the spout strikes the bottom and sides of the saucepan. The steam will condense to form droplets of water on the outside of the pan. These droplets will collect and fall like rain falling from a cloud.

3. Discuss how this experiment and the real formation of rain are alike.

Activity: **Rain**

Materials: (for each group)

- Science weather books or encyclopedia
- Narrow jar
- Marking pen or ruler

In the United States and around the world, technology is used to aid rain production. Children can find out about seeding clouds. They can research the different amounts of rainfall throughout the world. Use questions such as these when you discuss children's research.

- How does climate affect the condition of Earth?

- Are there any areas of Earth that are currently facing long-term droughts? What are some possible solutions to this problem?

- What are some ways water can be brought to dry areas?

The concept of irrigation can be introduced. Cities, such as Phoenix, Arizona, thrive because of irrigation. If water were not brought into this desert area, people could not live there. Crops could not be grown there. Managing the water supply was an art the settlers learned from the Mexicans, who learned it from the Pueblo Indians.

Children can use rain gauges to monitor the amount of rainfall at home or at school. To make a rain gauge, use a narrow vessel, such as an olive jar, marked on the outside to show fractions of an inch. Rainfall can also be measured by dipping a ruler into the jar.

Your students may be able to find weather pen pals from other areas of their city or state. By exchanging information with their new friends, students can develop a complete picture of the weather occurring in their area from a variety of sources. This project will help them realize that they cannot accurately judge the amount of rain by using only one source of data collection.

Meteorologists can speak to the class about tracking weather and forecasting future conditions. Amateur meteorologists often give valuable information about local conditions to professional weather forecasters on radio or television. Perhaps the students can compare their weather-tracking results with those produced by the meteorologist.

Activity: Rain Play

Materials: (for each group)

- Large piece of cardboard, plastic, or other sturdy material

Discuss with the children what they like to do on rainy days. In their neighborhood, what could they use, instead of a *yagua,* to slide down a hill? Let the children create an object (out of cardboard or other sturdy material) to experiment with. If no hill is available, perhaps the children can experiment with devices to help them slide on wet plastic.

Weather

Snow

LITERATURE

Coutant, H. *First Snow.* New York: Random House, Inc., 1974.

Lien is a Vietnamese girl who, having recently emigrated from tropical Vietnam, is excitedly waiting for the first New England snowfall.

Houston, J. *Long Claws: An Arctic Adventure.* New York: McElderry Books, 1981.

Two Inuit children summon up courage to face survival and a struggle with a bear.

Mendez, P. *The Black Snowman.* New York: Scholastic Inc., 1989.

This story is a touching tale of an African American boy who does not realize why he is unique and special. Through the magic of a beautiful African legend, the young boy finds inner strength and ability.

BACKGROUND INFORMATION

Water that freezes and crystallizes in the atmosphere is called *snow*. It may remain in the atmosphere, suspended in cloud formations, or it may fall to Earth and cover the ground for months at a time or, as in polar regions, form a permanent ice cap.

Snowflakes are collections of ice crystals, which appear in a variety of forms and often have intricate designs. The ice generally forms a six-sided structure because of the natural arrangement of atoms in the water crystal.

Discussion: The Black Snowman

Children can be motivated to learn about scientific concepts such as snow, crystals, and the weather through a book such as *The Black Snowman.* After reading the story, list all the questions the children may have about the story. Children can relate to feelings of being inadequate and unimportant at times. This story can generate interesting

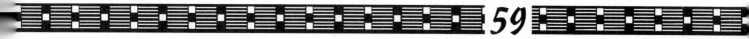

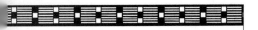

discussions about many issues. The following questions are examples of a type of inquiry that may be used to initiate an interesting science lesson: Why are snowflakes special? How are they made? Why was the snowman in the story black?

Activity: Crystals

Materials: (for each child or small group)

- Salt (rock, kosher, table, Epsom)
- Hand lens
- Black paper
- Paper and pencil

Let children examine substances that, like snowflakes, have six sides. When examining salt with a hand lens, it is more easily seen on a dark surface, such as black construction paper. Ask students to draw, in a science journal, each of the different types of crystals they observe.

Activity: Human Crystals

Materials: (for each child)

- Paper and pencil

Have students integrate a little drama into a lesson about snow. In groups of at least six, students can design and create their own unique human crystals by forming a repeated pattern with their arms and legs. They can do this activity standing, sitting, or even lying on the floor. After the students form their crystal, other students in the class may draw the human crystal they see for their science journals. Students can even think of a name to give each human crystal and record it in their journals, along with the picture.

LITERATURE

Kloben, H. and B. Day. *Hey, I'm Alive!* London: Curtis Brown, Ltd., 1963.

A plane crashes in the Alaskan wilderness. Two survivors have to stay alive for seven weeks before being rescued.

BACKGROUND INFORMATION

Weather

Insulation

In an igloo, some Inuit sleep on a low snow platform covered with twigs and caribou furs. Each igloo has a skylight made of freshwater ice. When summer arrives, the igloo melts, and the family moves into tents made of animal skins. In the western Arctic and in Greenland, some Inuit live in cabins made from driftwood and insulated on the outside with turf. Skylights are made from thin, translucent animal gut. These cabins are entered by way of a semi-underground passage that leads to a trapdoor in the floor. When summer arrives and the passageways are flooded, it is necessary to move into tents of seal or caribou skin.

Mammals have a number of traits designed to conserve heat energy. Most mammals have body hair, which insulates by trapping air. Instead of a hairy coat, water-dwelling mammals such as dolphins and whales have a thick, insulating layer of fat.

Discussion: *Hey, I'm Alive!*

What kind of material provides the best insulation? Before children answer this question, ask them to read *Hey, I'm Alive!* Discuss ways that insulation was used for survival.

Activity: Insulation

Materials: (for each group)

- Warm water
- Thermometer
- Paper cups
- Tape or rubber bands
- Variety of materials to test for insulating properties (aluminum foil, waxed paper, fake fur)

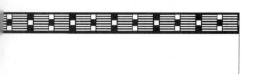

Children can test the insulating properties of a variety of materials by using them to insulate cups of warm water. Have children wrap materials around paper cups, holding them in place with tape or rubber bands. Have them include an uninsulated cup as a control. Then ask them to fill all the cups with warm water and measure the starting temperature. Ask children to predict which material will provide the best insulation. After 15–20 minutes, have children measure and record the temperature of the water in each cup. Ask: "Which material do you think will provide the best insulation? Think about the people who live in temperatures as low as –60° F. What kind of advice could you give them about their clothing choice in the Arctic winter? Think about animals that live in the North. What kinds of insulation did they use?" Help children design some experiments to compare different animals' insulation.

Activity: Ice-Cube Challenge

Materials: (for individuals or groups)

- Cardboard
- Fabric scraps
- Newspaper
- Aluminum foil
- Plastic wrap
- Plastic
- Ice cubes
- Paper and pencil

Give the following challenge to students: Can they think of a way to prevent an ice cube from melting? Allow children to work both in groups and individually to solve this problem. Students must create an insulating container for the ice cube. Remind children that an insulator is a poor conductor of heat. It keeps cold air near the ice cube and protects it from warmer air.

After groups have decided on a plan, ask them to draw their design to include in their science journals and explain why they think it will prevent the ice cube from melting. Then give each group an ice cube. (Make sure all the ice cubes are the same size.) Allow students to make their insulator. After one hour, check the ice cubes. Continue to check every half hour to determine which group has insulated their ice the best. The last ice cube to melt will win the contest for the group.

ETHNO SCIENCE FACT

Matthew Henson (1866–1955) was a great black explorer. He accompanied Robert E. Peary on many expeditions to the Arctic, beginning in 1891. In 1909 Henson, Peary, and four Inuit were the first people to reach the North Pole. Henson was the man chosen to plant the U.S. flag there.

Weather

Ice

LITERATURE

Houston, J. *Frozen Fire.* New York: McElderry, 1977.

This is a story of two boys, Matthew and Kayak, and their difficulties with surviving extreme cold.

Ullman, J. *Banner in the Sky.* New York: HarperCollins, 1954.

Rudi Matt was born in the Swiss village of Kurtal. He lives next to the Citadel and has ascended both the Dornel Glacier and the Blue Glacier.

Vizenor, G. "Almost a Whole Trickster," *A Gathering of Flowers,* ed. Joyce Carol Thomas. New York: Harper Collins, 1990.

When Pincher, Black Ice, and Uncle Almost decide to enter an ice-sculpture contest, they bring to life the folklore of their Chippewa ancestors.

BACKGROUND INFORMATION

When liquid water or water vapor becomes cold enough, it changes into solid water called *ice*. Ice is made up of crystals in various shapes. Liquid water freezes into six-sided needles. Most liquids contract as they freeze, but water expands. As ice forms on ponds, rivers, and lakes, it floats and forms a surface layer that helps keep water below it from freezing. Under this layer, some fish and other water animals stay alive.

Water vapor usually crystallizes on tiny solid particles, such as grains of dust. Cirrus clouds are made up of the microscopic particles formed when water vapor freezes. If there is enough water vapor in the air, these crystals grow into the complicated shapes of snowflakes. Hail is simply snow crystals partly melted and frozen again.

Activity: Freezing Salt Water

Materials: (for the teacher)

- Freezer

Materials: (for each individual or group)

- Measuring cup
- Measuring teaspoon
- Three identical paper cups, labeled *A, B,* and *C*
- Salt

Does salt water freeze? To help students answer this question, guide them through this simple experiment.

1. Put 1 cup of water in each of three identical paper cups.
2. Dissolve 16 teaspoons of salt in Cup B. Dissolve 3 teaspoons of salt in Cup C.
3. Store all three cups in the freezer overnight.
4. Take the cups out of the freezer. What do you observe? What can you conclude?

Activity: Expand or Contract?

Materials: (for the teacher)

- Refrigerator with a freezer compartment

Materials: (for each group)

- Two identical cans
- Water at room temperature

Safety: *If the can in the freezer has a tight stopper, the force will be great enough to split the can.*

Students can do this experiment to find the answer to this question: When water freezes, does it expand or contract? Guide the students through the following steps.

1. Fill the two cans exactly to the top.
2. Place one can in the freezer.
3. Place the second can in the refrigerator.
4. Let the cans stand until the next day (or until the one placed in the freezer is frozen).

The water placed in the cold (regular) compartment will have contracted so that it is not quite to the top of the can. The frozen water will have pushed out so that it extends above the top of the can. Why does this happen?

Ask the children to try to figure out their own explanation for this phenomenon. (Water expands when it freezes. During freezing, this expansion exerts extreme pressure.)

Activity: Ice All Around

Materials: (for the class)

- Water
- Ice-cube trays
- Plastic bags
- Freezer

With the children, observe icicles hanging from a building. If students live in a location where they do not see icicles, bring in large photographs or take the children on a field trip to an underground cavern. Encourage the children to note the different shapes. Bring an icicle into the classroom for the children to handle and watch melt. Brainstorm with children about the different uses of ice. Freeze some ice for classroom purposes. Use a plastic bag and water to make an ice pack for injuries, make ice cubes for beverages, make ice to use in making ice cream with the children.

Weather

Wind

LITERATURE

McKissack, P. *Mirandy and Brother Wind.* New York: Knopf, 1988.

In this African-American story, Mirandy attempts to capture the wind in order to win first prize in the Junior Cakewalk.

Walter, M. *Brother to the Wind.* New York: Lothrop, Lee & Shepard Books, 1985.

An African folk tale about Young Emeke who risks dishonor with his tribe because of his lifelong dream to fly—which he is able to do by making a special kite.

Yolen, J. and E. Young. *The Girl Who Loved the Wind.* New York: Harper Trophy, 1987.

A widowed merchant tries to protect his beautiful daughter from unhappiness and, in so doing, virtually makes her a prisoner.

BACKGROUND INFORMATION

Wind has a great effect on climate and weather. Wind changes the face of the Earth. Winds, like water, constantly wear down rocks and create canyons. The wind can carry away sand and soil. This is called wind erosion.

Activity: Weather Vane

Materials: (for each child or small group)

- Wooden stick, 1-in. square × 12-in. long
- Cardboard
- Scissors
- Metal washer
- Short piece of metal tubing
- Nail, smaller than hole in stick
- Block of wood
- Hammer

Ahead of time: *Drill a hole in the center of the 12-inch stick. Cut a slit in each end of the stick. The slits should be going the same direction.*

Safety: *Closely supervise children when they work with the nails. You may want to do the hammering yourself.*

Assist children in making a weather vane to detect wind direction. A simple one looks like an arrow mounted on a base. A stick of wood with a hole drilled in the center is the main part of the weather vane.

1. Have children cut out a cardboard pointer to fit into a slit at one end of the stick, and a "feather" of cardboard to fit into the slit at the other end. The feather must be larger than the pointer so that it will catch the wind.

2. Next, have children place a washer on top of the hole in the stick and drop a loose-fitting nail through the washer.

3. Show children how to place a short piece of metal tubing over the lower end of the nail before the nail is pounded into a wooden, stationary mounting.

4. Place the weather vane where it will catch the wind. When the wind blows, the stick pivots on the nail until the pointer faces into the wind.

Weather Vane

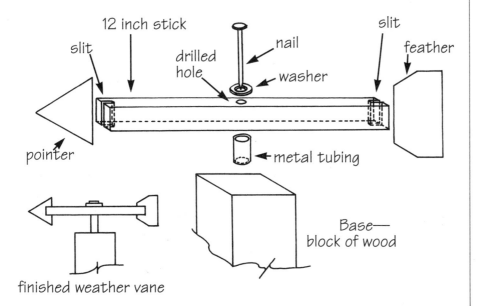

Activity: Wind Socks

Materials: (for each child)

- A 28-in. × 22-in. sheet of newspaper
- Crayons or markers
- Watercolors and brush
- Glue
- Tape
- String
- Staples
- Scissors
- Extra newspaper

Guide the children with the following directions for making wind socks.

1. Show the students how to fold 1 full sheet of newspaper (28 inches by 22 inches) in half lengthwise.

2. Encourage them to draw a fish form and cut out the shape, without cutting on the fold.

3. Next, have students open the newspaper and draw scales and eyes. After the drawing is complete, students can paint over it with watercolors. Let it dry overnight.

4. Have students fold back the mouth edge about 1 inch twice and glue it down.

5. Then have students tape the string along the length of the mouth.

6. Next, fold the fish back together. The students should place crinkled-up newspaper inside the fish and staple it shut.

7. Last, have the students attach string to the edges of the mouth, and hang it where the wind will catch it.

Wind Sock

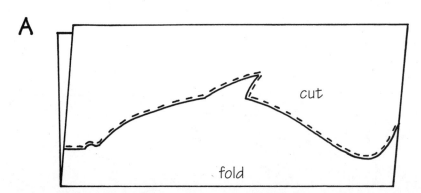

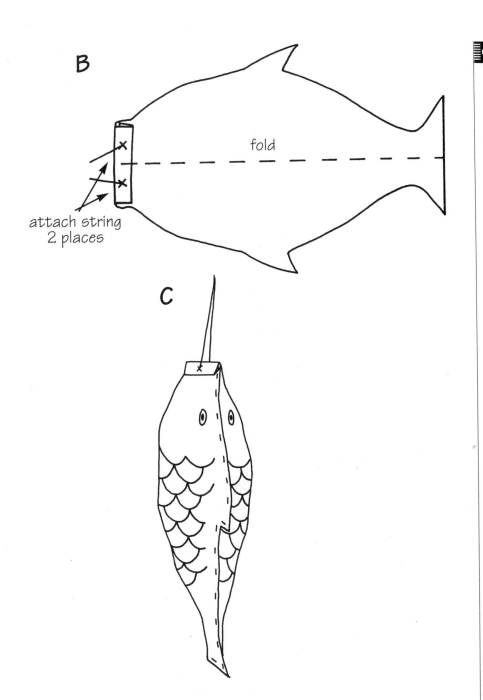

B

fold

attach string
2 places

C

Activity: Sand Dunes

Materials: (for the class)

- Electric fan
- Sand
- Materials to make fences and walls
- Safety glasses for each child

Safety: Closely supervise children when the electric fan is on. Be sure that each child wears safety glasses.

Wind can make sand dunes and snow dunes during the winter. Help children figure out a way to make a miniature sand dune with an electric fan. How do fences, walls, and other similar objects affect the formation of these dunes?

Activity: **Wind Projects**

Materials:

- Feathers, corks, plasticine shapes, paper, balloons, parachutes, shuttlecocks
- Paint, brushes, crayons, fabric markers, paper, fabric, pulleys, string
- Light cardboard, paint, brushes
- Nontoxic powdered paint, water, drinking straws, paper

1. Observe the movement of things through the air. Take the students outside during a windy day to drop things, such as feathers, and watch how they fall.

2. Design flags. Use paint and crayons with paper, and fabric markers to decorate fabrics. Encourage students to make flags from different countries that they may be studying. As an extension, challenge students to consider how the flag could be attached to a flagpole. Perhaps they can design a pulley system to fly their flag. The flag pole and pulley could be a small version that could fit on top of their desk, or could be larger.

3. Make and decorate a fan. Look at a collection of fans from different countries. All kinds of decorations can be used—folding, cutting, water color, embroidery, and so on. Students might collect pictures from magazines of people in different countries holding and using fans. They can try to imitate some of the designs they see.

4. Make "blown" pictures. Students can use straws to blow dry powder (mixed with water) and paint pictures. Instruct children to keep turning the paper while they are blowing the paint.

Safety: Be sure children understand that they are not to get paint in their mouths.

Weather
Clouds

LITERATURE

Ginsburg, M. *How the Sun Was Brought Back to the Sky.*
New York: Macmillan, 1975.

A Slovenian folk tale that tells of the sun and involves animal characters. The story includes an important role for clouds.

BACKGROUND INFORMATION

Clouds are collections of water droplets, ice crystals, or mixtures of both. People observe the shapes of clouds in the sky. Farmers and sailors have relied on weather to help them predict the coming of storms.

Cloud classification is divided into high, middle, and low. The names of the 10 categories of clouds are derived from combinations of three primary classifications of clouds: cirrus, stratus, and cumulus, with the addition of the words *alto* for high clouds and *nimbus* for rain clouds.

Activity: Clouds

Materials: (for the teacher)

- Hot water
- Glass bottle
- Thin piece of cloth
- Rubber band
- Crushed ice

Pour hot (not boiling) water into a glass bottle. When the bottle becomes hot, pour out all but one inch of water. Next, stretch a thin piece of cloth over the mouth of the bottle and fasten it with a rubber band. Place crushed ice on top of the cloth. Have students observe the cloud that forms as the warm air meets the cold.

Activity: Fog

Materials: (for the teacher)

- Matches

Materials: (for each child or small group)

- Clear plastic soft-drink bottle with cap
- Warm water
- Bright window or lamp

Ask children to review the process of forming clouds. What two things are needed for clouds to form? (Tiny particles, such as dust, soot, or pollen; and warm, moist air that is cooled.) Students (with careful teacher supervision) can make their own fog in a bottle.

1. Fill the bottom of a clear plastic soft-drink bottle with 1 inch of warm water.

2. Lay the bottle on its side. Have the teacher light a match and, after it burns for a couple of seconds, blow it out.

3. A student can hold the match in the opening of the bottle so that smoke drifts into the bottle.

4. Screw the cap on the bottle. Swish the water around to rinse all parts of the bottle.

5. Hold the bottle up toward a bright window or lamp. Squeeze the bottle for a moment and then let it go. What do you see inside the bottle? You should see a faint fog. How is this like a cloud in the sky? What happens each time you squeeze and release the bottle? Why does this fog continue to form?

Activity: Cotton Clouds

Materials: (for each child)

- Construction paper
- Glue
- Cotton
- Black marker

Have students fold a piece of construction paper into fourths. In each section, have them glue one type of cloud made out of cotton. For dark rain clouds, students can color the cotton with a black marker. They can identify the name of each of the clouds under each picture. They can also make a display of cotton clouds that are in different shapes. Students can have fun trying to guess what shapes the other students in the class made.

LITERATURE

Millhoff, K., A. Griese, A. Borgo, et. al. *Gift from the Storm and Other Stories of Children Around the World.* Honesdale, Pennsylvania: Boyds Mills Press, 1993.

A typhoon hits the island of Saipan. The child in the story must accept losses and understand nonmaterialistic rewards that a crisis situation can give. "Gift from the Storm" is the first story in this compilation of multicultural stories.

Stolz, M. *Storm in the Night.* New York: HarperCollins Publisher, 1988.

During a storm, this African American family explores the sights and sounds they experience without electricity.

Wartski, M. *A Boat to Nowhere.* Louisville, Kentucky: Westminster John Knox Press, 1980.

Mai and her family escape from their Vietnamese village and are able to survive storms at sea in a struggle to stay alive.

Weather
Storms

BACKGROUND INFORMATION

The term *storm* usually is used to describe the following destructive or unpleasant weather conditions: strong winds, heavy rain, snow, sleet, hail, lightning, or a combination. All storms (thunderstorms, cyclones and tornadoes, hurricanes and typhoons) follow a cycle and occur only in a specific season, when the atmosphere has all the right elements necessary for them to happen.

Activity: Tornado

Materials: (for each child or group)

- Tornado tube (sold in teacher-supply stores)
- Two 2-liter soft-drink bottles

Help students use a tornado tube and two 2-liter soft-drink bottles to simulate a tornado.

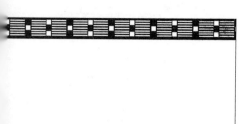

ETHNO SCIENCE FACT

Tropical hurricanes have been the focus of studies by Hispanic American meteorologist José Angel Colon (b. 1921). Dr. Colon has also served as chief forecaster of the U. S. Weather Bureau in San Juan, Puerto Rico.

If you are using a commercially-made tornado tube, you will need two plastic two-liter soda bottles. Fill one of the bottles 2/3 full with water and screw the tornado tube onto this bottle. Screw the other bottle to the other end of the tornado tube. To begin the vortex action, turn the entire assembly so that the full bottle is on top. Hold securely and shake the upper bottle briefly in a circular motion while holding the bottom of the assembly still. You might wish to add glitter or use colored water.

Activity: Hurricanes

Materials: (for the class)

- Chart paper and markers
- Videotaped weather reports with hurricane information

Children can track hurricanes on their own chart as they view radar reports given out by weather stations. They can make predictions as to how long the hurricane will last and where it will go next. Bring in videotaped weather reports to test children's predictions.

Tornado Tube

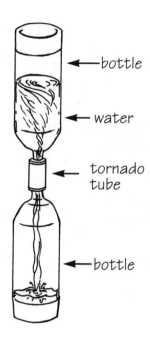

← bottle

← water

← tornado tube

← bottle

Activity: Historic Storms

Materials: (for the class)

- Weather books or encyclopedias

Have children research historic storms to find answers to questions such as these: Where and when were the highest waves? The most damage from one tornado?

Students can also interview family and friends. They can ask them if they were ever in a tornado or hurricane. What was it like?

Activity: Lightning

Materials: (for each small group)

- Comb
- Piece of wool or fur
- Metal doorknob, or other metal object

Tell students that they can make their own special type of lightning. The students need to rub a comb with a piece of wool or fur and hold it near a metal doorknob. A small spark will be produced. After producing the spark, have the students compare this to what happens in nature.

Activity: Thunderstorm

Tell students that they are going to create something that will sound like a thunderstorm. Try to do this activity in a gym. Have the students sit on the floor and begin by closing their eyes and becoming absolutely quiet. When it is completely quiet, begin rubbing your palms together. When the student to the left of you hears the sound, he or she will join in, and so on. When everyone is making this sound, make the storm grow louder by snapping your fingers. After everyone is snapping, slap your thighs to make the sound of heavy rain. Thunder can be added by stomping feet. After the storm reaches its peak, calm it down by reversing the order of the noises, until complete silence is reached.

Shinto is the ancient Japanese religion based on nature. Believing that rocks, trees, mountains, and winds have spirits, the ancient Japanese instituted rituals and ceremonies to honor nature. Native Americans also have, at the center of their personal philosophy, a deep respect for all living things. To Native Americans, each animal, tree, and manifestation of nature had its own spirit. They believe in living in harmony with all things.

Activity: **Four Seasons**

Materials:

- Recording of Vivaldi's *Four Seasons*
- Tape recorder, or CD player
- Construction paper for each child
- Crayons or markers

Play Vivaldi's *Four Seasons* for the students. As they listen to it, encourage them to close their eyes and picture what they hear. Then discuss the types of instruments heard. Ask questions such as: "Why were those instruments and sounds heard during that season? What types of weather were represented by the sounds and instruments?" Allow the students to listen to the recording again, and instruct them to draw the scenes they imagine from the mood of the music on large sheets of construction paper folded in fourths.

UNIT 4

MAMMALS

MAMMALS

Wolves

LITERATURE

George, J. *Julie of the Wolves.* New York: Harper & Row, 1972.

Miyax runs away and becomes lost in the Alaskan wilderness, without food or even a compass. She becomes accepted by a pack of Arctic wolves and draws upon their help and love to survive.

Goble, P. *Dream Wolf.* New York: Bradbury Press, 1990.

This is a Plains Indian legend about becoming lost in the hills. Tiblo and Tanksi depend on a mysterious night visitor to help them.

BACKGROUND INFORMATION

The wolf is a highly intelligent and courageous hunter. Its remarkable powers of endurance are legendary. Wolves belong to the same family as dogs and coyotes. Only two species of wolves remain today—the gray wolf and the red wolf. Because of human persecution and habitat destruction, the gray wolf, once among the most widespread mammals outside the tropics, is now found in substantial numbers only in a few regions in Europe, Asia, and North America. The pure red wolf is thought to be almost extinct in the wild.

For centuries, the wolf has been a symbol of courage and endurance. North American Indians use the name of the wolf for their most powerful warriors. There have been many stories of wolves that have raised human children from infancy, as in the famous story of Romulus and Remus.

When two wolves have a disagreement, they may bare their teeth and snarl at each other. Both wolves try to look as fierce as they can. Usually, the less dominant wolf gives up before a fight actually takes place. To show that it gives up, the wolf rolls over on its back. The other wolf stands over it.

Wolves are very good at showing other wolves how they feel about things. They often use their faces and ears to express their feelings. To show anger, a wolf may stick its ears straight up and bare its teeth. Suspicion is shown by pulling the ears back and squinting. When a wolf is afraid, it may flatten its ears against its head.

Discussion: Julie of the Wolves

Read *Julie of the Wolves* aloud to students. Throughout reading the book, bring up the following examples of how life in Alaska can be very different from the experiences the students have.

Since Julie is lost, how can she measure time and distance without a clock or measuring tool? In the story, students might remember that Julie uses phrases, such as "two sleeps ago," to measure time. To measure distance, she uses the measurement of "many harpoon shots away." To find a direction, Julie keeps a close eye on the north star. Ask the students to figure out how this would help her. Also, Julie watches for clues so she remembers where she has been before. What are these clues (noticing certain flowers and plants, watching for plants that have been stepped on, and so on)?

In this book, animal communication patterns can be found throughout. How does Julie understand the wolves? What signals does she first identify? (For example, a sign of friendship is a pat on the chin.)

Julie thinks about the food chains she observes in the wilderness. What are some examples? (Grass—rodents—snowy owl—weasel—white fox) Why does Julie refer to nighttime as "wolf time"?

Activity: Wolf Ears

Materials: (for half the class)

- Blindfolds

This activity will help children find out how wolves can locate the source of a sound by turning their ears. First, ask half of the students to put on blindfolds. Have each blindfolded student ask a partner to stand on the other side of the room and clap his or her hands. The blindfolded students should turn their heads back and forth until the sound is loudest, and point their fingers in the direction from which the sound seems to be coming. The students should then take off the blindfolds and see if the direction was correct. Next, tell students to put the blindfolds back on. They should ask their partners to move around the room, one at a time, clapping. See if the blindfolded students can follow the movements by turning their heads.

Students can practice imitating the non-verbal communication of wolves. They can each invent their own personal signals to indicate various emotions or feelings, such as happiness, hunger, sleepiness, sadness, and so on. They must demonstrate their signals to another person in the room to see if that person can guess what the emotion or feeling is.

LITERATURE

Dupre, R. *Agassu: Legend of the Leopard King.* Minneapolis: Carolrhoda, 1993.

In this West African tale, Agassu frees himself of his chains and becomes the leader of his people.

Lester, J. *How Many Spots Does a Leopard Have? And Other Tales.* New York: Scholastic Inc., 1989.

This book includes ten African and two Jewish folk tales.

Newton, D. *Spider and the Sky God.* Mahwah, New Jersey: Troll Associates, 1993.

A spider uses trickery to capture the four prizes demanded by the Sky God in payment for his stories. One of the major characters in the story is a foolish leopard. This is a legend of the Akan people in West Africa.

BACKGROUND INFORMATION

The leopard usually lives in Africa, Asia Minor, Central Asia, and the Far East. It is a large cat, closely related to the lion, tiger, ocelot, panther, and cheetah. The leopard is normally a buff color with dark spots. It lives in bush and forest areas. It is agile, can climb trees, and is a remarkable jumper. Normally active at night, it attacks antelope, young cattle, and pigs.

Activity: Big Cats

Materials: (for the teacher)

- Pictures of big cats: leopards, lions, tigers, ocelots, panthers, and cheetahs

Materials: (for each child)

- Drawing paper
- Crayons or markers

Show children pictures of big cats. Ask students to consider the following questions: "How are these animals similar? What characteristics do they have in common? How do they differ from one another?"

Students can make drawings of leopards blending in with their environment while doing what they are good at—climbing, jumping, running, and hunting.

Activity: Leopard Spots

Materials: (for the teacher)

- Large sheet of butcher paper
- Black construction paper
- Tape

Ahead of time: *Draw a life-size outline of a tiger on butcher paper. Cut out black spots from construction paper, and place a circle of tape on the back of each spot.*

Divide the class into two or three teams. Have each student run up and place a spot on the leopard and then return to the back of the line. The team that has attached the most spots in 2 minutes wins.

Activity: Leopard Olympics

Materials: (for the class)

- Large boxes
- Small ladders
- Other obstacles

Help students create an obstacle course patterned after a make-believe forest. Students need to use boxes, ladders, and other obstacles to simulate objects that could be found in a jungle—trees, small hills, vines, boulders, streams, and so on. After the obstacle course is created, students can enjoy competing as individuals or teams to complete it in record time.

LITERATURE

Carpenter, F. "The Shah Weaves a Rug," *The Elephant's Bathtub.* New York: Doubleday, 1962.

An Iranian folk tale about a ruler in Persia who finds a very clever solution to a challenge. In this tale, it is discovered why Persian rugs are still valued throughout the world.

Goble, P. *The Great Race of the Birds and Animals.* New York: Bradbury, 1985.

This is a Cheyenne myth in which the Creator has a race to see which animals will rule the world—two-legged or four-legged animals.

Palacios, A. *The Llama's Secret.* Mahwah, New Jersey: Troll Associates, 1993.

This is a Peruvian legend of the Great Flood story, in which a llama warns the people and animals to seek shelter.

BACKGROUND INFORMATION

One of the early Spanish explorers wrote of seeing 20,000 llamas in one herd. It is estimated that as many as 300,000 llamas were being used at that time to transport silver ore from the mines of the Incas. Llamas are still very abundant. Large flocks are raised in the Andes Mountains from southern Peru to northwestern Argentina. The female llama usually bears one young each year.

The llama is primarily a pack animal, but it is also valuable as a source of food, wool, hides, tallow for candles, and dried dung for fuel. Llamas can carry up to 210 pounds. Although they usually move slowly, they can make marches of up to 16 miles a day. When overloaded or exhausted, however, a llama will lie down, hiss, spit, kick, and refuse to go on.

Llama wool is spun on a hand spindle that the American Indians have used for hundreds of years. The wool varies in color, being a light brown, occasionally spotted with dark brown or black. It is woven into a warm cloth.

MAMMALS

Llamas

Activity: Dyeing Wool and Cotton

Materials: (for the teacher)

- Shallow glass pan, or disposable plastic pan
- Water
- Spoon or stick for mixing

Materials: (for each child or small group)

- Raw wool
- Raw cotton
- Hand lens
- Nontoxic fabric dye
- Plants for dyeing (optional)

Ahead of time: *If the fabric dye you are using requires mixing, do the mixing yourself ahead of time.*

Obtain samples of raw wool and raw cotton. Give children hand lenses to analyze the samples. Encourage students to think about all the products that are made out of wool and cotton.

Allow children to use a small amount of fabric dye to color the raw cotton and wool. Ask them to think about other ways to color cotton and wool besides using dye. Native Americans have used plants and other natural substances to dye products. What are some of these plants? Plants such as rabbitbrush, wild onion, cliffrose, sumac, juniper, walnuts, and dock can be used to dye wool.

Students can experiment with plants to try to dye some of their wool and cotton samples.

Activity: Llamas and Camels

Llamas belong to the same family of animals as camels. Ask children to describe similar and different characteristics of both animals. Which animal would be easier to ride? Why? Students can pretend they are llamas. What advantages would a long neck provide? How do humans carry heavy objects? If they were llamas, how might they carry heavy loads? Ask children to walk like llamas while carrying books on their backs. Is it hard to walk around like this? Would it help to have a long neck and long legs?

Activity: Walking Like an Animal

After reading *The Great Race of the Birds and Animals,* have children think about their own lives. How would their daily activities be different if they walked on their feet and hands? What could they do better? What kinds of activities would be more difficult? Children can have races matched up with other classmates in the following configurations: regular race (not paired with anyone), three-legged (two people with one leg each tied together), four-legged (three people with middle person tied to two other people). Students can have fun racing with each other and figuring out the best techniques to use to make their constraints work.

MAMMALS

Elephants

LITERATURE

Harill, J. *Sato and the Elephants*. New York: Lothrop, 1993.

This tale was inspired by the true story of a Japanese ivory carver who refused to use ivory to carve when he discovered the source.

Wolkstein, D. *8,000 Stones: A Chinese Folktale*. New York: Doubleday, 1972.

A small boy helps his ruler by figuring out how to weigh an elephant.

BACKGROUND INFORMATION

The largest living land animal is the elephant. The great size of adult elephants and the thickness and toughness of their skins protect them from other wild animals. Since they have no enemies to fear except humans, elephants are usually peaceful and easygoing. The relationship between humans and the elephant is referred to in mythology. In India, the Hindu religion has an elephant-faced god named Ganesha. There is a Hindu legend that says that, long ago, elephants had the power of flight, but lost it when they landed on a banyan tree and fell through to crush the house of a hermit. As a result, the hermit's curse grounded them forever.

Elephants have an average life span of 70 years. Elephants are not usually afraid of mice. What they seem to fear is getting some small object stuck in their trunks. Elephants show great affection for one another and spend their lives as members of a family herd.

Big animals need large amounts of food, and the elephant is the biggest eater of all. An elephant's digestive system is not very efficient. In general, it digests only half of the food the animal eats. As a result, elephants actually eat twice the amount of food that their bodies need.

Discussion: Living As Elephants

Ask students to pretend that they are the largest living land animal on Earth. As elephants, they need to find a herd to belong to. Instruct the students to get into groups of 5–8. Inform them that they are now a herd. They will be very kind to each other and do everything together for the rest of their lives (which might be as long as 70 years). Ask them, as a group, to decide on answers for the following questions.

- Where are we going to live? By a river? In a desert? In a jungle?

- What will we eat? Who will do the hunting?

- What happens when there is danger? Who will send out a signal? How will we send each other signals? How will we communicate (without talking)?

- What will happen when one of us is sick? Should we take him or her along with us if we have to move? Should we wait for anyone if we are in danger?

- What should we do with the babies in the herd? Who should watch them? How will we protect them from danger? What should we teach them?

Each group of students should keep track of their decisions on these questions. Children might even enjoy writing their own play about what life would be like as elephants.

Activity: Human and Elephant Diets

Share this information with the class.

In the course of a year at a zoo, an elephant:
- Drinks 15,500 gallons of water.
- Eats 1,600 loaves of bread.
- Eats 100,000 pounds of hay.
- Eats 12,000 pounds of dried alfalfa.
- Eats 1,500 gallons of mixed grains.
- Eats 2,000 potatoes.
- Eats 3,000 cabbages, apples, carrots, and other vegetables.

To compare the eating habits of a human child and an elephant, ask the children to gather data for one week on what they eat each day. They should each keep a simple food diary in which they can record everything that they eat and drink throughout the day. After one week, students should total and divide their data into different categories of food and drink. They should multiply their data by 52 to represent what they would consume in one year. After finishing this assignment, students should provide answers to the following questions.

- How many gallons of liquid do you consume each day? Each week? Each year?

- How many pieces of bread do you eat each day? For this exercise, count 20 pieces of bread as one loaf of bread. How many loaves of bread do you eat each day? Each week? Each year?

- How many potatoes do you eat each day? Each week? Each year? Remember to count French fries, hash browns, and mashed potatoes. (Help children estimate how many French fries would equal a whole potato).

- How many apples, carrots, bananas, celery, and other fruits and vegetables do you consume each day? Each week? Each year?

Ask the children to compare their data with that of an average elephant. Which items in their diet are different? Which items are the same? Could they eat the same amount as an elephant? Why or why not? How are our digestive systems different from those of elephants?

MAMMALS

Horses

LITERATURE

Cohen, C. *Mud Pony.* New York: Scholastic Inc., 1988.

This is a story about a poor boy who wanted a pony. He made one out of mud. He had a dream that his pony was alive and, when he woke up, it had come to life.

Goble, P. *The Girl Who Loved Wild Horses.* New York: Macmillan, 1982.

A young girl loves horses and is able to communicate with them in special ways.

Yep, L. "The Magical Horse," *Tell Me a Tale.* Lexington, Massachusetts: D. C. Heath and Company, 1995.

A special horse can carry its rider far beyond his dreams.

Yolen, J. *Sky Dogs.* San Diego: Harcourt Brace Jovanovich, 1990.

This is a story of Native Americans called Blackfeet who were known as the "people of many horses." This tells the story of how the people saw horses for the first time.

BACKGROUND INFORMATION

Of all the animals, the horse has probably shared the most human adventures. The horse has also been associated with human progress. For thousands of years, the horse has participated in the pleasures, the dangers, and the hard work that have marked human life. No one knows exactly when people and horses first became companions. Some historians believe that people probably hunted early horses, as they did other game animals. Drawings, engravings, and sculptures of horses that date back many thousands of years may have been made by hunters and medicine men as offerings to the gods for a good hunt. At some point in time, people recognized the advantage of the horse's fleetness, tamed the horse, and used it to pursue other animals for food. When food became scarce in one area, the horse helped people move and settle in other areas that were more productive.

Gradually, people found more and more uses for the horse and became increasingly dependent upon it. As this dependence grew, the horse became a partner in human life. The horse also made possible many pleasures. Pride in this magnificent animal has prompted people to show it off in horse shows, and admiration for the animal's beauty and grace has inspired its portrayal in art and literature.

Until the early 1900s, the horse was an important part of everyday life. Then machines began to perform many of the jobs that horses had done, and the population of horses dropped drastically.

Activity: Horse Lineage

Students can trace the lineage of a show horse. A guest speaker can come to the class to discuss the business of raising and selling horses. A horse's family heritage can be shown to the class and discussed.

Activity: Horses on Tiptoe

Horses walk on tiptoes. Students will have fun thinking about this concept. In a simple activity, ask the children to stand, walk, sit, and run on their tiptoes for a while. Was it difficult for humans to do this? What does a horse's foot look like? Why does it have such a hard hoof? What would happen if humans had hard hooves, too? What could we do differently?

Activity: Horses vs. Machines

Materials: (for the class or each small group)

- Chart paper
- Marker

Children can make a chart to show how the horse was used before and after the early 1900s. What were horses used for? What did we make to replace them? How would our society today be different if we used horses more? What would be better (or worse) if we rode horses instead of driving cars? Students can write a play to demonstrate how life today would be different if horses were used more and other machines were used less.

UNIT 5
REPTILES

REPTILES

Snakes

LITERATURE

Aardema, V. *Why Mosquitoes Buzz in People's Ears.* New York: Dial Books for Young Readers, 1975.

This is a West African tale about mosquitoes.

Ata, T. *Baby Rattlesnake.* Chicago: Children's Book Press, 1989.

This is a traditional Chickasaw story about a rattlesnake who wants to grow up quickly.

Morgan, W. "Coyote and Snake," *Navajo Coyote Tales.* Santa Fe, New Mexico: Ancient City Press, 1988.

This is a Native American folk tale that explains why coyotes and snakes are not friends.

BACKGROUND INFORMATION

People have been awed and fascinated by snakes. Their fears and misunderstandings have resulted in numerous myths. It has been said, for example, that snakes use their tails to whip people, and can shape themselves into hoops to roll down hills. Snakes are not capable of either of these feats!

Snakes are reptiles and are closely related to lizards. There are more than 2,000 species of snakes.

Many people associate snakes with painful and venomous bites. A snake will bite a human only when it is frightened or threatened. In rural areas, snakes serve a useful purpose because they feed on animals, such as rats and mice, that are generally considered to be pests.

Although international laws place restrictions on the capture and transport of many species of snakes, some continue to be hunted as a source of leather or to be sold as pets. Members of venomous species are captured and kept in captivity for the production of antivenin. Many larger snakes are edible by humans, and provide a source of food in parts of Asia.

Activity: A Snake

Materials: (for the teacher)

- Recording of animal sounds (optional)
- Tape recorder, or CD player (optional)

Materials: (for each child)

- One long, white tube sock
- Markers
- Glue
- Pink felt
- Two small, black sequins
- One knee-high stocking

Art projects can be integrated into science. For example, children can make their own snakes by decorating socks with markers. A small bit of felt can be glued near the mouth for a tongue, and sequins glued on for eyes. The sock then becomes a puppet with which to read a story about snakes and reptiles.

Snakes shed their skin. This can be demonstrated by pulling the knee-high stocking over the sock (while the child is using it as a puppet). Snakes become dull in color just as the puppet did. Further discussions can occur on behaviors of snakes, what they like to eat, where they live, and which are poisonous.

Why Mosquitoes Buzz in People's Ears uses the sounds each animal makes within the story. Children can listen to recordings of various animal sounds and identify the animals they hear. They can also try to make their own recordings of animal sounds.

Activity: Howdy, Snake!

Materials: (for the class)

- Large, glass tank with 2 to 2 1/2 inches of sand in the bottom
- Water in a small pan (no deeper than the sand)
- Branched sticks
- Rocks
- Wire mesh screen, larger than the top of the tank
- Two books

If possible, try to get a small, tame snake for the children to examine. A local pet store may help you with this. Let the children touch it and discover that it has dry, cool skin, rather than a slimy coating. Children can learn that most of the snakes in this country are very helpful to humans, and that snakes consume many thousands of destructive rodents and insects each year. This activity will help students learn to have respect for snakes. Caution the class never to hunt for snakes unless accompanied by a responsible and informed adult. Show them pictures of poisonous snakes, which would include the rattlesnake, copperhead, water moccasin, and coral snake. Help the class build a little snake habitat by completing the following steps.

1. Cover the bottom of a large glass tank with about 2 1/2 inches of sand.
2. Push down a small pan of water so it is even with the sand surface.
3. Add a branched stick and some rocks to the tank.
4. Put the snake inside.
5. Cover the tank with a wire mesh screen that overlaps. Turn it down on all sides. Use two books to weigh it down.
6. Watch the snake from time to time. Handle it no more than twice a day. (Hold it just behind the head. Support the body with your other hand.)

Discuss questions such as these.

- What are the snake's eyes like? Can you see eyelids? Does it blink?
- How does its skin feel?
- How does it move? Climb?
- How does it drink?
- How does it take its food? (Put a meal worm or earthworm into the cage and watch). Note: Some snakes will not eat in captivity. After several weeks, they should be returned to their original habitat.
- What else do you observe about the snake?

REPTILES

Iguanas

LITERATURE

Mike, J. and C. Reasoner. *Opossum and the Great Firemaker.* Mahwah, New Jersey: Troll Associates, 1993. Little Opossum learns a lesson trying to steal fire from the Great Iguana in this Mexican legend.

BACKGROUND INFORMATION

Iguanas differ greatly in their looks and habits. Most of them are green. Some take on the color of their surroundings. Many of them have unusual sawlike teeth. They also have large pouches under the head and neck; and long, scaly crests all along the back.

Most iguanas are found in the Western Hemisphere. Included in the iguana family are the chameleons of the southwestern United States. The common iguana of Central and South America grows seven feet long and may weigh up to 30 pounds. It lives in trees, where it sprawls out on a branch with its legs dangling. It feeds on leaves and other plants.

Activity: **Insect Hunt**

Materials: (for the teacher)

- A dozen or more pictures of insects

Ahead of time: *Hide the pictures of insects around the room or out on the playground.*

Explain to children that some animals prefer to hunt alone and some like to hunt in packs. Ask students to think of animals that might be included in these two categories. Tell them that animals, such as foxes or bobcats, like to hunt alone and will not attack an animal larger than themselves. Ask students to think of a reason why a fox or bobcat would prefer to hunt smaller animals when alone. Explain that the other group of animals, pack hunters, will take on prey much bigger than any single member of the pack. Animals in this category include wolves and lions.

Ask students to predict which category iguanas would belong to. Inform them that young iguanas have been observed leaving their nest area and traveling through their environment with others to hunt for insects. They will hunt as a pack rather than alone. Discuss the advantages iguanas would have as they hunt together. Are there any disadvantages?

To explore this concept, tell students that they are going to go on a scavenger hunt. Students should find as many insect pictures as possible in 10 minutes.

The class should go on the scavenger hunt twice. The first time should be as individuals. The second time, they should be placed in groups of 4 to 6 students. Ask students to compare the number of insect pictures they find as individuals and as members of a group. If they were young iguanas, would they have found more insects hunting alone or with the group? In what ways did group members help each other? Were there any dangers for the group?

Activity: Camouflage

Materials: (for each child)

- White paper plate
- Markers in different colors
- White plastic spoon

Iguanas and chameleons are able to adapt to their environment through the use of camouflage. There are many activities that can help children understand the concept of camouflage. One is to allow children to create a design of their own on the back side of a white paper plate with colored markers. Next, they can make a matching design on the back rounded side of a white plastic spoon. They are to make the spoon design in such a way that it hides the spoon on the plate, when seen from a distance. After they complete this, students should switch their spoons with other classmates and discuss what they see. Is their own spoon or their friend's spoon more easily seen on their own plate? Why? How is this similar to the way a chameleon blends into the surrounding environment? What would happen if a green chameleon did not turn brown when it was on brown soil?

Children can also discuss how other animals protect themselves if they cannot change their colors. How do humans protect themselves?

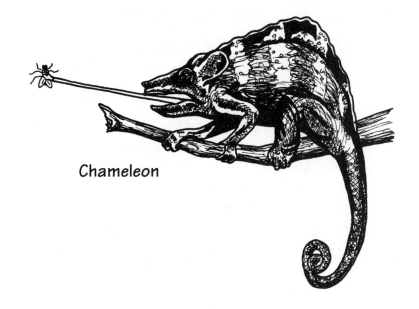

Chameleon

LITERATURE

Kerr-Wilson, B. *Turtle and the Island.* London: Frances Lincoln, 1990.

A great sea turtle longs to find land so she can rest. The sea turtle builds up an island, which is called Papua, New Guinea.

Mollel, T. *The King and the Tortoise.* New York: Clarion, 1993.

The King in this Cameroon folk tale challenges the animals in his kingdom to prove their wisdom.

REPTILES

Turtles

BACKGROUND INFORMATION

Turtles are reptiles. Reptiles are cold-blooded. They are covered with scales and breathe air with lungs. They usually lay hard- or soft-shelled eggs. Turtles live mostly on land. They have feet with toes and claws. The painted turtle is one of the more common species. It has a bright yellow and red edge on its shell and often basks in the sun. The musk turtle is also common.

Activity: **Turtle Learning Centers**

To help children explore various characteristics of reptiles and turtles, set up four learning centers or stations around the classroom. Each station will help students understand one particular concept about reptiles and turtles. The stations should be set up as described below.

Learning Center 1: Scales and Slime

Materials:

- A piece of clay with rows of seeds stuck in it (labeled *A*)

- A piece of cellophane covered with a thin layer of vegetable oil (labeled *B*)

- Paper and pencil

Students should feel material A and then material B. Write a short list of words that describe how each material feels.

Which one represents reptile skin, and which one represents amphibian skin? (Material A represents reptile skin, and B represents amphibian skin.)

Learning Center 2: Eggs
Materials:

- Tapioca sprinkled in a container filled with water (labeled *A*).

- A few grapes laid on dirt (labeled *B*).

Students should feel the material floating in A and the objects in B. Describe some differences between them. Which ones represent amphibian eggs, and which ones represent reptile eggs? (Tapioca represents amphibian eggs, and grapes represent reptile eggs).

Learning Center 3: Changing Colors
Materials:

- A black pipe cleaner taped to a piece of black construction paper (labeled *A*)

- A yellow pipe cleaner taped to a piece of black construction paper (labeled *B*)

Ahead of time: *Tape A and B to a wall about 8 feet away from the station.*

Ask students to look at both papers with pipe cleaners. Which is harder to see, the black pipe cleaner or the yellow pipe cleaner? The colors of some reptiles and amphibians can change. For example, a chameleon can change from green to brown. How might this help it to survive?

Learning Center 4: Backbones

Ask students to reach around and feel the middle of their backs. What bones do they feel? Which of the groups listed below have similar bones in their backs?

- Frogs
- Lizards
- Ants
- Snakes

(All vertebrates, including all reptiles and amphibians, have backbones and internal skeletons.)

Aruego, J. and A. Aruego. *A Crocodile's Tale.* New York: Scholastic Book Services, 1972.

This is a Philippine folk story that features a conversation between a crocodile and a little boy.

Bush, T. *Three at Sea.* New York: Crown, 1994.

This is the adventure that occurs as an inner-tube drifts down a river to the sea. The story also involves dolphins, turtles, and crocodiles. The issue of endangered species is present throughout the story.

de Paola, T. *Bill and Pete.* New York: Putnam & Grosset, 1992.

Bill, the crocodile, and Pete, the bird, have adventures together along the banks of the River Nile.

BACKGROUND INFORMATION

The alligator and the crocodile share many characteristics and are easily confused. Both have long, powerful bodies carried close to the ground on their short legs. Their tails have lots of strong muscles to help them swim; they also use them as weapons to defend themselves. Their thick, scaly hides also help protect them from the attacks of other animals. Their long jaws are lined with sharp teeth to grab prey. Their eyes, ears, and nostrils are located on the tops of their heads so they may hide under water but still be able to see, breathe, and hear above the surface of the water.

Alligators and crocodiles lay eggs. Mother crocodiles and alligators usually carry their newly-hatched young to the water by carrying them in their mouths. Both alligators and crocodiles eat small animals, such as reptiles, amphibians, fish, birds, and mammals. Sometimes they catch larger animals, but they cannot swallow them whole.

How can you tell an alligator from a crocodile? An alligator has a rounded snout at the end of its face; the crocodile's face is pointed. When an alligator is grown up, you cannot see any of its teeth when its mouth is closed;

you can see the crocodile's fourth tooth on either side of its jaw when its mouth is closed.

Crocodile

Alligator

Activity: Puppets

Materials: (for each child)

- Small paper bag
- Glue
- Crayons or markers
- Construction paper
- Yarn scraps
- Scissors

Encourage the children to find out information about various types of alligators and crocodiles. Give each student a small paper bag. Tell the students to use their glue, crayons or markers, construction paper, and yarn scraps to create a bag puppet of an alligator or crocodile. When the students show their puppets to the class, have them tell why they like that animal. Also, they can share other information about where the animal is normally found. Information about the country, climate, and people can also be included.

UNIT 6

BIRDS

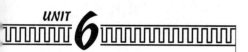

Crows

LITERATURE

Morgan, W. "Coyote and Crow," *Navajo Coyote Tales.*
Santa Fe, New Mexico: Ancient City Press, 1988.
This is a Native American folk tale about the trick a crow played on a hungry coyote.

Yashima, T. *Crow Boy.* New York: Puffin, 1976.
Chibi does not fit in with his classmates at school because they think he is too different. Finally, at the talent show, Chibi makes friends by sharing his wonderful ability to make crow sounds.

BACKGROUND INFORMATION

Crows are large, loud-calling birds with strong bills. The males help build their nests and feed their young. Crows live on all of the continents that are not very cold and on most large islands.

The common American crow is a glossy, black bird about 20 inches in length with a fan-shaped tail. Its usual call is a loud "caw-caw." It lives in all of eastern and most of western North America. This crow's habitat includes wooded areas, farmland, and even suburban areas. It is found as far north as the Arctic Circle and as far south as Florida, the Gulf Coast, and northern Mexico. Crows do not migrate long distances, but thousands will sometimes spend their nights at a common center, dispersing each morning to their feeding grounds.

Because they like to eat a wide variety of plant and animal foods, crows are a nuisance to farmers and compete with other wildlife for food. Crows feed on agricultural crops such as fruits, corn, and other grains. They also consume enormous numbers of insects, including harmful pests. They have also been known to eat baby birds, rabbits, mice, and snakes.

Crows are considered to be among the most intelligent birds. Some young crows will become entertaining pets and can be taught to perform simple tricks. Pet crows have even been taught to talk like parrots. They are also thieves that will steal any little trinket or shiny object, a trait that must be guarded against in a household with a pet crow.

Discussion: Crow Boy

After reading *Crow Boy*, students can try to imitate all the different crow sounds they read about in the book. Why do birds sound different at different times? How do birds and other animals communicate? Children can research the answer to these and other questions before doing further activities.

Activity: Animal Talent Show

After children have researched a number of animals and their communication patterns, they can choose one to specialize in. They will need to try and visit a zoo, rent a video, or listen to a tape to actually hear the animal they wish to imitate. After several weeks of practicing and experimenting, the class can have its own talent show like the one in *Crow Boy*. After each student demonstrates his or her animal sound, classmates must guess which animal is being portrayed. In addition to making the animal sounds, students can act out the animal's unique behavior or design puppets to use. You may wish to take the class on tour to other classrooms to demonstrate the different animal sounds.

Activity: Origami

Materials:

- Books on origami
- Colored paper

You may wish to integrate art into a lesson on birds and other animals by using the Japanese art of origami, or paper folding. This form of art is almost 1,000 years old. It is inexpensive and colorful. Japanese children make origami as gifts and decorations, and they use it to practice eye-hand coordination. There are many books which contain directions and examples on how to make different birds and objects.

Swallows

LITERATURE

Ishii, M. *The Tongue-Cut Sparrow.* New York: Lodestar/E. P. Dutton, 1986.

A peasant's wife drives away the sparrow that is her husband's best friend.

Newton, P. *The Five Sparrows.* New York: Atheneum, 1982.

A Japanese tale of how a kind woman rescues an injured sparrow and nurses it back to health.

Politi, L. *Song of the Swallows.* New York: Macmillan, 1948.

Every summer, the swallows leave San Juan Capistrano and fly away. They always return in the spring on St. Joseph's Day. In the story, Juan plants a garden and hopes for the swallows to nest there.

BACKGROUND INFORMATION

More than one third of the world's bird species migrate with the seasons. You can tell swallows are getting ready to migrate when they line up in the thousands on telephone wires. Most birds migrate from the north in the fall. Cold winters pose a problem to birds because food isn't as available as it is in warm weather. The days become shorter in winter, which means that birds have less time to hunt for food and need to use more energy to keep warm. Migration is very risky and millions of birds never reach their destinations. (The most orderly migrators are lobsters, which march single file along the seabed, each lobster keeping in feeler contact with the lobster ahead.)

Discussion: Song of the Swallows

After reading the story, children can discuss migration and other unique patterns of behavior that animals may have. How would the swallows find their way back to San Juan Capistrano? Ask students, if they had to pick a second place to live each year, where would it be? Also, if they were not able to ask for directions or to have a map, how could they find their way between the two locations?

Activity: Migration

Somewhere at school, establish a race track at least 50 meters long. The goal of this activity is to get people to migrate from their northern/summer home (start) to their southern/winter home (finish).

To begin with, everyone lines up at the starting line. A leader calls out the name of an animal. Everyone must race to the finish line like the animal called. For example, if the chosen animal is a duck, everyone waddles to the finish line. The first duck to reach the winter home is the Great Duck.

You or an assigned leader may start with birds, since they are the most common migrators. Next, the class can explore the behavior of other animals that migrate (for example, snakes, worms, fish, wild dogs, kangaroos, turtles, hares, lobsters). As a variation, you can mix different animals in the same race.

After this activity, students should have a basic understanding of migration. The following activity can demonstrate the dangers involved in migration. As before, mark the racing course, but this time also set boundaries at the sides. Three-quarters of the children should run the race; the rest should act as obstacles. The obstacle people stand in the race course. While keeping their left foot planted in one spot, they try to tag the migrators. If tagged, a migrator "dies" by stopping in place or falling to the ground.

Activity: Bird Walk

Materials: (for each child)

- Two empty toilet-paper tubes
- Tape

Ahead of time: *Make pretend binoculars by taping two toilet-paper tubes together.*

Give the children the pretend binoculars, and take them on a bird walk. Pick a spot to sit outside to watch the birds. Children may take along a science journal to record their observations. Encourage students to describe the birds' sizes, beak shapes, colors, ways of moving (walking, hopping, running, flying), songs, and calls.

Activity: Bird Feeders

Materials: (for the teacher)

- Pictures of bird feeders

Materials: (for each child)

- Empty milk carton
- String
- Scissors
- Craft stick for spreading peanut butter
- Pine cone
- Peanut butter
- Birdseed

With the children, look at pictures of different kinds of bird feeders and discuss what kinds of foods attract birds. Have students make bird feeders from milk cartons, following these directions.

1. Poke a hole in each side of the milk carton, near the top. Put string through the holes, so the bird feeder can be hung on a tree.

2. Cut an opening at the bottom of one side of the milk carton.

3. Make a snack for the birds by spreading peanut butter on a pine cone, rolling it in bird seed, and placing it inside the opening at the bottom of the milk carton.

4. Hang the bird feeder on a tree.

As an experiment children may try different types of seeds and predict which ones will be the most popular. Perhaps they will be able to notice if certain species of birds tend to prefer a specific type of seed.

Bird Feeder

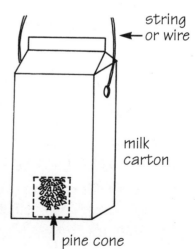

string or wire

milk carton

pine cone

Activity: Bird Feathers

Materials: (for each small group)

- Variety of bird feathers (The education specialist at a zoo may be able to help you get these.)
- Hand lens
- Pan of water

Ask the children to use a hand lens to examine the feathers, noting the differences between tail or wing feathers and downy fluffs. See if feathers will float. Talk about why they float. What are feathers for?

Owls

LITERATURE

Edmiston, J. *Little Eagle Lots of Owls.* Boston: Houghton Mifflin Co., 1993.

Little Eagle Lots of Owls is given a wonderful gift by his grandfather to help him remember his full name.

Gates, F. *Owl Eyes.* New York: Lothrop, 1994.

This is a traditional Kanienkihaka-Mohawk legend about how owls came to look as they do.

BACKGROUND INFORMATION

Owls can be found in many places: prairies, savannas, taiga, Arctic and subarctic snowfields and forests, northern and temperate coniferous and deciduous forests, deserts, swampy grasslands, subtropical forests, and marshes.

While owls are known for their silent flight, some of them make special noises when the occasion demands. An owl's feathers enable it to fly without any sound.

Their offset ears and highly developed sense of hearing enable the nocturnal owls to attack in total darkness. The flat facial disk is covered with wiry feathers which radiate from the center of the face outward and serve to channel sound to the ears. These feathers are also extremely sensitive to the minute and delicate movement of sound waves passing through the air caused by prey moving about far below.

Owls hear in an unusual way. Sound waves enter one ear, travel through an air passage, and exit out the other ear, hitting each ear drum on both sides. While much is made of the owls' hearing, it is their vision they most rely upon, especially the nocturnal owls. Owls are unable to move their eyes. So, to keep its eye on a moving shape, an owl must turn its head. It can turn its head around almost 180 degrees until it is pointing almost straight back behind it. To see the rest of the view, the owl whips its head around in the other direction, again almost 180 degrees from the front of its body.

Many birds must eat one quarter or more of their body weight in food each day. Owls need to fly to find enough food, while the reason they need so much food is to power their flight. A delicate balance must be struck between the energy used to find food and the energy gained to stay alive.

Activity: Owl Hunt

Materials: (for each child)

- Blindfold

Safety: *You may wish to have older students help guide blindfolded children.*

Divide the class into groups. One group will act like owls, one group will be insects, another group will be large mammals, and one group will be rodents. Each group should decide on a distinctive sound. Everyone should be blindfolded. Without speaking, the owl group must locate the rodent group and decide whether or not to hunt for it.

Discussion: Food Comparison

Ask: "Do we need food for energy? How much food do we eat? What percentage of our own body weight do we eat? How can we figure this out? How does this compare with the amount of food owls eat?"

Hawks

LITERATURE

Baylor, B. *Hawk, I'm Your Brother.* New York: Scribner's, 1976.

Rudy struggles to tame a wild hawk and learns to fly.

BACKGROUND INFORMATION

Hawks are often mistaken for eagles. Hawks are sometimes used as trained hunting birds. They live in wooded areas, often near water. A typical hawk builds a platform nest, usually in a tree; lays one to five eggs; and feeds on birds, mammals, and occasionally frogs and insects. Although hawks are agile, successful hunters, they will sometimes feed on another animals' leftovers.

Activity: Food Chain

Materials:

• Cards, one for each child

Ahead of time: *On each card, write one of the parts of the food chain: sun, plant, insect, frog, snake, hawk.*

Hawks are part of a food chain that begins with plants. Plants need the sun to grow. Many insects eat plants, many toads eat insects, many snakes eat toads, and many hawks eat snakes.

Students can use this activity to explore what happens when a food chain is broken. After the students are introduced to the idea of what a food chain is, they can do the following dramatization. Divide the class into groups of seven.

1. Have each child pin a card to her or his clothes.
2. Students should stand in line and hold hands in this order: sun, plant, insect, frog, snake, hawk.
3. Have students act out the answers to these questions by sitting down when their part of the food chain is eliminated.

- What animal would die if there were no snakes to eat? (The snake person should drop hands and sit down.)
- What animals would die if there were no frogs to eat? (The frog person drops hands and sits down.)
- What animals would die if there were no insects to eat? (Insect person drops hands and sits down.)
- What animals would die if there were no plants to eat? (Plant person drops hands and sits down.)
- What would happen if there were no sun to let plants grow?

After this activity, discuss different types of food chains. Older children might connect two or more food chains to make a more complicated food web. Students can even run strings among individuals in the web to show the complex interrelationships involved.

Activity: Eyes

Materials: (for each child)

- Black construction paper or fabric
- Elastic
- Staples

Materials: (for pairs of students)

- Soft ball

Ask: "Do you think birds have good vision?" To explore the answer to this question, first draw an outline of a bird's head on the board. Tell students that most birds have eyes on the sides of their heads. In some birds, like the owl and hawk, the eyes face forward. Ask a student to come to the board and draw in the hawk's eyes.

Next, have each person compare human eyes with the eyes of a hawk. Like a hawk, our eyes face forward. Explain that people have binocular vision, which means both eyes focus on the same image. Birds usually have

monocular vision because each eye focuses on a different image. Most birds have binocular vision only when they focus straight ahead, with both eyes on the same image.

Ask students to gently shut one eye or cover one eye with a hand and look around. Ask if they can tell a difference between one-eyed sight and two-eyed sight. Do they think that animals with binocular vision can judge distance better than those with monocular vision? Why?

To answer this question, have students make an eye patch using a piece of black construction paper or fabric stapled to an elastic band. Ask students to form a large circle and play catch. First, have them play catch without the eye patch on. Then ask everyone to cover one eye with a patch. After playing catch for a few minutes, ask students to compare the level of difficulty in catching a ball with and without the patch. Ask them to analyze the hunting skills of a hawk. Why is a hawk (and an owl) such a good hunter?

LITERATURE

Polacco, P. *Rechenka's Eggs.* New York: Philomel Books, 1988.

This is a special story of Babushka and eggs.

Walker, A. "Why Did the Balinese Chicken Cross the Road?" *Living by the Word.* San Diego: Harcourt Brace Jovanovich, Inc., 1988.

An essay which argues that human beings must live in harmony with the world around them.

Yoshiko, U. *The Rooster Who Understood Japanese.* New York: Scribner's, 1976.

Mrs. Kitamura owns a loud rooster, and a little girl helps her find a good home for it.

Young, E. *The Rooster's Horns.* New York: Philomel Books, 1978.

The story takes place in China. It tells why the vain Rooster no longer wears his horns and how Dragon and Worm trick him.

BACKGROUND INFORMATION

Chickens belong to the order of heavy-bodied birds adapted to life on the ground. Chickens have difficulty with long-distance flight because they have short wings. Their legs and toes are adapted for running and scratching.

The domestic chicken has a short, curved beak and strong feet. Both the male and the female have one or two wattles. Wattles are fleshy growths that hang from the chin or throat. A male chicken also has a large comb, or crest, of similar tissue.

There are 225 varieties of large chickens and 107 varieties of small chickens. Small chickens are called bantams.

BIRDS

Chickens

Activity: Egg Incubation

Materials: (for small groups)

- Fresh egg
- Small bowl

Materials: (for the class)

- Pan of water
- Container to protect eggs
- Eight fertilized eggs
- Incubator
- Overhead projector
- Drawing paper and pencils

Safety: *Have children wash their hands after handling eggs or chicks.*

Divide the class into cooperative-learning groups, and give each group one fresh egg. Have students break the fresh egg into a bowl and examine the egg for its main parts (shell, yolk, albumen, air sac). Discuss the function of each part. (The shell is needed for protection, the yolk provides food, the albumen provides water, and the air sac provides air.)

Next, discuss what an egg must have from its environment in order to hatch and how the students are going to meet these needs by using an incubator.

- A pan of water will provide the needed moisture.
- A light (temperature should be 100 degrees Fahrenheit) will provide warmth for the eggs.
- The container will protect the eggs.
- Students will rotate the eggs.

Before beginning, work with the class to decide what they will do with the chicks once they are hatched. Also, prepare students for the possibility of some of the eggs not hatching. The students (with parents' permission) may wish to take a chick home and raise it there. However, you may find other homes for the chicks.

To start the incubation process, guide students through the following steps.

1. Place 8 fertilized eggs in incubator.

2. Place a small pan of water inside incubator to keep eggs moist.

3. Mark eggs lightly with pencil or crayons so that, when eggs are rotated daily, positions will be noted.

4. Turn the incubator on.

5. Regulate temperature to about 100 degrees Fahrenheit (39 degrees Celsius).

6. Rotate eggs daily about one-third of the way around.

7. Check temperature and moisture daily.

8. Between the seventh and tenth days, eggs can be "candled." (Candling is observing the inside of eggs with the aid of a strong light.) Use an overhead projector for the strong light. Study the eggs. Draw sketches of observations.

9. Between the seventeenth and twentieth days, eggs should be candled again. Study the eggs. Draw sketches of observations.

10. Around the twenty-first day, the eggs will hatch at various intervals of time. The chicks will peck their way through the eggshells. Students will probably be able to hear the chicks before they actually see them come out of their shells.

Hummingbirds

LITERATURE

Belpre, P. "The Legend of the Hummingbird." *Tales from Here and There.* Lexington, Massachusetts: D. C. Heath and Company, 1995.

This is a Puerto Rican folk tale about how two lovers are changed into a flower and a hummingbird.

Ferreira, F. *Feathers Like a Rainbow: An Amazon Indian Tale.* New York: Harper & Row, 1989.

The birds in the forests surrounding the Amazon River have dark feathers until they decide to steal some colors from the hummingbird.

Palacios, A. *The Hummingbird King.* Mahwah, New Jersey: Troll Associates, 1993.

A beautiful hummingbird blesses the birth of a special child in this Guatemalan legend.

BACKGROUND INFORMATION

The Portuguese call it *beija-flor*, meaning "kiss-flower." The Aztecs adorned Montezuma's ceremonial cloaks with its feathers. The dazzling hummingbird still captures people's fancy. Because of special flight muscles that control wing beats of 38 to 78 times per second, a hummingbird can hover in the air and is the only bird that can fly backward. The smallest hummingbirds can attain wing-beat frequencies of 200 per second during courtship flights, when the males show off their brilliant plumage. Hummingbirds drink nectar at the rate of about 13 licks per second. They also eat insects. The giant hummingbird, 8 inches long, lives at altitudes of 15,000 feet in the Andes Mountains. The Cuban bee hummingbird is the smallest bird in the world, measuring 2 1/4 inches.

Activity: **What Hummingbirds Do**

Materials: (for each child)

- Red fruit punch in a plastic cup
- Pencil and paper

Materials: (for the class)

- Scale

A hummingbird can outfly any insect or bird in the sky. Children can see how many times they can move their arms up and down (to simulate flapping wings) in one minute. Compare that number to what a hummingbird can do— up to 200 times per second! Ask children to consider how small the hummingbird is. Why do hummingbirds move so quickly? Would they move as quickly if they were much larger?

The tiny bird needs a lot of energy to keep going. It sips half its own weight in nectar each day. Give each student red fruit punch in a plastic cup. Have children try to see how many times they can lick the punch. Compare their number of times with what a hummingbird can do— 13 licks per second!

Ask students to weigh themselves and write the number that would be half their weight. This number represents the amount of food they would eat each day, if they were hummingbirds. Encourage students to make lists of foods (and their weights) that they would have to eat to equal half their weight each day.

Activity: Hummingbird Feeder

Materials: (for the class or small groups)

- Red paper or fabric
- Tall, thin, tubular container
- Tape
- Small stick
- Honey
- Paper and pencils
- Warm water
- Red food coloring
- Plain, unsweetened water (optional)
- Blue food coloring (optional)

Help children make a hummingbird feeder, following these steps.

1. Hummingbirds love red flowers. They love petunias, morning glories, and snapdragons. Children can make a large red flower (out of paper or red fabric) to tape near the end of a tall, thin, tubular container. Place the flower about 1 cm from the open end.

2. Tape this feeder to a small stick, and push the stick into the ground. Make sure that it is placed among some flowers.

3. Make a honey solution to fill the feeder. This solution should be one part honey to three parts warm water. Add one or two drops of red food coloring. Stir well before pouring it into the feeder.

4. Students should check the level of the solution every few days.

Ask the children to think of reasons why a hummingbird might prefer red, sweet liquid to drink. How is this liquid similar to the nectar in brightly colored flowers? Students can keep a journal to track the behavior of the hummingbirds.

As a variation in this experiment, ask the children to put plain, unsweetened water in the feeder. Does the behavior of the hummingbirds change? What happens if students use plain water that is not colored red? What happens if the water is blue?

UNIT 7

Insects & SPIDERS

Insects
& SPIDERS

Spiders

LITERATURE

Arkhurst, J. "Why Spider Lives in Ceilings," *The Adventures of Spider.* Boston: Little, Brown and Company, 1964.

A West African folk tale that explains how a clever spider locates a warm and safe place to escape becoming a meal for a leopard.

Haley, G. *A Story, A Story: An African Tale.* New York: Macmillan, 1970.

Anansi, the Spider man, wants all the stories in the world. He sends three sly creatures to get them.

McDermott, *Anansi the Spider.* New York: Henry Holt & Co., 1972.

Anansi is a folk hero of the Ashanti people of Africa. This book combines two legends to create a fun and interesting look at human qualities.

BACKGROUND INFORMATION

The word *spider* derives from an Old English verb *spinnan*, meaning "to spin." People of European descent tend to dislike spiders. In many African and North and South American cultures, spiders are revered. They play a large role in controlling populations of insects, including those insects that cause human disease. Spiders can live and adapt to many different and diverse habitats.

Discussion: Anansi the Spider

Children are fascinated by spiders and insects. There are many sources of multicultural literature that integrates with this topic. To begin to understand spiders, children can first observe a spider (in a glass-enclosed aquarium) and record what they see. They can watch how a spider spins a web. Many questions surface while observing a spider? How does a spider eat? How does it trap small insects? After the actual experience, children are ready to do something more abstract. Read *Anansi the Spider* to the class. There are many legends involving Anansi. Through the adventures of Anansi, we can explore human emotions and solutions to problems presented in the story. Children can relate their discussion to what they have already learned about spiders. They can talk about the meaning of the legend of Anansi and how it relates to real spiders.

Activity: Spider Web

Materials: (for each child)

- Picture of a spider web (See *Ahead of time*)
- Black paper
- Tape
- Pencil with sharp point
- White yarn
- Black and red pipe cleaners
- Velcro™ (the hook side)
- Waxed paper
- Staples

Ahead of time: *Draw a spider web, and duplicate copies.*

Give materials to each student. Help children follow these directions to make spider webs.

1. Put the spider-web picture on top of the black paper, and tape the two together.

2. Use a pencil to punch holes through both papers at regular intervals along the outline for the web.

3. Weave white yarn in and out through the holes that have been punched, following the design on the web picture. When finished, tear off the top paper and a white web will be visible.

4. For the spider, intertwine black or red pipe cleaners. Place the spider in the center of the web.

5. For a "victim," take a small amount of Velcro and fold it into a ball. Cut tiny wings out of waxed paper. Staple the wings to the Velcro. This represents a fly. Children can use the fly (and make others) to throw onto the web (the Velcro will stick).

Activity: Spider Collection

Materials:

- Glass or plastic jar, with holes in the lid
- Materials to provide an environment for spiders (similar to those in the area where it is found)

Safety: *If you live in an area where poisonous spiders live (such as black widows), explain the dangers.*

With adult supervision, children can collect different kinds of spiders. You need to carefully explain guidelines to children on how to do this. A class field trip would be a good way to handle this. After obtaining a spider, students should provide an environment for it similar to the area where it was found. By observing and caring for these spiders, children will learn a great deal about their unique qualities.

Activity: String Web

Materials: (for the teacher)

- Nails
- Hammer

Materials: (for the class)

- Sturdy string
- Materials, such as pipe cleaners, to make spiders

Ahead of time: *In a large, out-of-the-way location, hammer four or five nails in a pattern to form supports for a string web.*

Safety: *Do not have the students do the nailing.*

In addition to the yarn web, children can build their own spider webs with string. Again, this activity requires adult supervision.

1. Use sturdy string and prepare the outside frame.
2. Next, make the spokes tying the ends to the frame. Don't make it too tight or too loose. Tie the starting

string in the center and go round and round toward the outside, wrapping around each spoke that you pass. Use lengths of string that the children can manage. When the end of the string is reached, it should be tied to the closest spoke.

3. Tie the next string to the same spoke that you left off with, and continue in this manner until the web looks the way you want it to.

4. Make spiders, insects, an egg sac, and baby spiders to attach to the web.

Spider Web

Moths

LITERATURE

Caduto, M. and J. Bruchac. "Moth, the Fire Dancer," *Keepers of the Night.* Golden, Colorado: Fulcrum Publishing, 1994.

This is a Native American explanation of why moths are attracted to bright lights.

Demi. *Demi's Secret Garden.* New York: Holt, 1993.

Twenty poems on insects are presented and illustrated with collages.

BACKGROUND INFORMATION

Moths belong to a group of insects whose name, *Lepidoptera*, means "scale wings." They are so named because their wings and certain portions of their bodies are covered with a fine "dust." Under a microscope, the dust is seen to be made up of millions of finely ridged scales that are arranged in overlapping rows. The beautiful colors and markings of the insect are due to the scales, which come in a remarkable variety of colors.

Butterflies and moths look very much alike. The best way to tell them apart is to examine their antennae, or feelers. Butterfly antennae are slender, and the ends are rounded into little clubs or knobs. Moth antennae lack these knobs. Their antennae usually look like tiny feathers.

Moths fly at night. Moths rest with their wings outspread. Different kinds of moths live in many places throughout the world. They vary in size from 10 inches from tip to tip of the spread wings, to only 1/5-inch across. In North America, there are 8,000 kinds of moths.

Like all insects, moths have three pairs of legs and a body that is divided into three sections—head, thorax, and abdomen. On the thorax, or middle section of the body, are two pairs of wings. The pair in front is usually the larger. The scales on the wings contain a pigment that gives the insect some of its color.

These insects feed on the nectar of flowers and on other plant liquids. The mouth is a long slender sucking tube. By uncoiling the tube, the insect probes deep into the flowers and sucks up the nectar.

A moth's antennae are very sensitive to odors. Some males can detect a particular scent of a female from over six miles away. Thus, the sense of smell is extremely important to moths.

Activity: Insects' Attraction to Light

Materials: (for the class or small groups)

- A light source
- Colored cellophane
- Paper and pencil

Children can develop an experiment to find out which color light attracts insects the most. This would be a good activity to assign as homework. Children can wrap different colored cellophane around lights. After taking the lights outside at night, students can carefully observe and record the number of insects that circle around each light.

Activity: Scents

Materials: (for each group)

- Empty baby-food jars
- A different scent for each student in a group (vanilla, cinnamon, spices, fruit, perfume, potpourri, for example)

Ahead of time: Punch holes in the lids of baby-food jars. Place a different scent in pairs of baby-food jars. If you are using solids instead of liquid extracts for the scents, paint or wrap paper around the jars to mask their looks.

Divide the students into two groups. Give each person in one of the groups a small baby food jar that contains a scent. Give students time to memorize the scent, then take their jars away. Give matching scent jars to the second group to walk around the room with. Challenge group one students to find their scent "mates." Moths can find their mates in the dark, by using only their sense of smell.

Insects & SPIDERS

Caterpillars & Butterflies

LITERATURE

Merrill, J. and F. Cooper. *The Girl Who Loved Caterpillars.* New York: Putnam, 1992.

Izumi resists social and family pressures as she befriends caterpillars and other socially unacceptable creatures.

White Deer of Autumn. *The Great Change.* Oregon: Beyond Words Publishing, 1992.

This is a sensitive book about life and death. In this story, Native American children deal with the mystery of change in people and in animals. The process of a caterpillar becoming a butterfly is discussed.

BACKGROUND INFORMATION

Butterfly antennae are slender, and the ends are rounded into little clubs or knobs. Most butterflies fly and feed during the daytime. Butterflies rest with their wings held upright over their backs. In North America (north of Mexico), there are 700 kinds of butterflies.

Butterflies have three pairs of legs and a body that is divided into three sections—head, thorax, and abdomen. On the thorax, or middle section of the body, are two pairs of wings. Like moths, these insects feed on the nectar of flowers and on other plant liquids.

Activity: Life Cycle of a Butterfly

Materials: (for the class)

- Large, plastic container with a hole cut in the lid
- Dark-colored netting
- Glue
- Caterpillar
- Paper towels
- Small, wide-mouthed jar
- Leaves
- Paper and pencil

Ahead of time: Cut a hole in the lid of the plastic container, leaving about one inch of plastic around the rim. Cut a piece of dark-colored netting, and glue it under the rim of the lid.

After reading a story, such as *The Great Change*, the children may be motivated to keep several caterpillars in their classroom. Students may find caterpillars outside on young milkweed plants (Monarchs), under the leaves of carrot and parsley plants (Black Swallowtails), or on the ground in wooded areas (Woolybear caterpillars). The following hints may help students have a successful experience.

1. Put a paper towel and the leaves in the wide-mouthed jar. Place the jar in a corner of the plastic container.
2. Put the caterpillar in the plastic container with the air vent in the top.
3. Keep the caterpillar well fed with fresh leaves.
4. Clean out droppings daily. A paper towel on the bottom of the food jar provides easy cleanup.
5. Don't place the caterpillar in direct sunlight.

Children can watch the caterpillar and record what it does and eats each day. They can record information such as:

- The appearance and size of the caterpillar.
- The color of the chrysalis or cocoon.
- How much the caterpillar eats.
- What happens each day—what behavior is observed.
- Length of time it takes the butterfly to come out of the chrysalis or cocoon.

The children will become excited when they observe the caterpillar spinning the cocoon and disappearing within it. They can record carefully, make drawings, and take pictures of the process.

One day, students will be able to witness the butterfly emerge. They must be careful not to touch the butterfly during this process. Also, they must be aware that this may occur when they are out of the room (during the night when they are not at school). They can also discuss where to release the butterfly once it has emerged.

Insects & SPIDERS

Crickets

LITERATURE

Porte, B. and D. Ruff. *"Leave That Cricket Be, Alan Lee."* New York: Greenwillow, 1993.

Alan Lee tries to catch the singing cricket in his mother's office, after hearing the Chinese legend of the insect from his great-uncle.

Selden, G. *Cricket in Times Square.* New York: Farrar, Straus, & Giroux, 1960.

Chester, a cricket, takes up residence in a Times Square newsstand with a mouse and a cat. Together, they befriend Mario and his family.

BACKGROUND INFORMATION

About 1,000 kinds of crickets have been discovered by scientists. Even though they have hard, shiny wing covers across their backs, they do not fly. Crickets have a pair of long, slender antennae. Crickets can be very quick and can jump long distances.

The common field cricket of the United States is black and about 1-inch long, with antennae longer than its body. Crickets eat plants, but they will occasionally eat other small insects. Crickets live beneath rocks, wood, or other debris. They usually dig a burrow that is used for shelter when they are not feeding.

A newly-hatched cricket is called a nymph. It looks like the adult, but it has no wings. Nymphs grow in a series of molts, during which they grow out of their skin, emerging slightly larger after each shedding.

Tree crickets are light green and are among the most persistent noise makers. The chirps of crickets slow down as the temperature drops.

Activity: Crickets

Materials: (for the class)

- Clear, plastic shoe box
- Dry soil
- Small bowl to fit in the shoe box
- Water
- Torn paper towels
- Dry oatmeal
- Raisins
- Crickets (See below.)
- Screen
- Hand lens

Encourage children to catch some crickets to study in their classroom. If children are unable to catch crickets in fields, they may be purchased at fish-bait stores. Try to obtain both male and female crickets. From egg to adult takes about six months. Adults live about three months.

After the crickets have been obtained, students can proceed to make a home for their crickets.

1. Put about 2 1/2 inches of dry soil in a plastic shoe box.

2. To provide a female a place to lay eggs, fill a bowl with soil. Sprinkle water on it until it is all damp. Bury it in the dry soil so that the damp soil is even with the dry soil.

3. For a place to hide, scatter some pieces of torn paper towel around the container.

4. Scatter some dry oatmeal and a few raisins at one end.

5. Put no more than three or four crickets inside the container.

6. Cover it with a screen large enough to fit as a tight lid on the shoe box.

After giving students time to observe the crickets, lead them through an inquiry lesson. This type of lesson might include the following questions.

- How do the crickets act?
- How do they use the pieces of paper toweling?
- How do the crickets eat?

- How do the females lay eggs?
- What happens when cricket eggs hatch? What do the young (nymphs) look like? What do they look like as they get older? (Use a hand lens to help you see.)
- What else can you observe about the crickets?

Activity: Chirp Time

Materials:

- Crickets

Children can estimate the temperature by listening to the sound of crickets. Children should count the number of chirps they hear from crickets in one minute. Divide this number by four and then add the number 40. The result should be the temperature in degrees Fahrenheit.

UNIT 8

GROWING THINGS

GROWING THINGS

Plants

LITERATURE

de Paola, T. *The Legend of the Bluebonnet.* New York: G. P. Putnam's Sons, 1983.

This is a Comanche Indian legend that tells how the bluebonnet, the state flower of Texas, came to be. This flower was a sign of forgiveness from the Great Spirits.

Garland, S. and T. Kivchi. *The Lotus Seed.* San Diego: Harcourt Brace Jovanovich, 1993.

A young Vietnamese girl saves a lotus seed and carries it everywhere to remember her homeland.

BACKGROUND INFORMATION

Most plants are green. They all have roots, a stem, and leaves; some have flowers and seeds. We like to eat different parts of the plant. We eat leaves when we eat spinach, lettuce, and cabbage. We eat flowers when we eat broccoli and cauliflower. We eat stems when we eat asparagus and potatoes. We eat roots when we eat carrots, radishes, turnips, and beets. We eat fruit when we eat apples, corn, cucumbers, and pineapples. We eat seeds when we eat peanuts, walnuts, popcorn, wheat, and rice.

Activity: **Liquids in Plants**

Materials: (for the teacher)

- Knife

Materials: (for each small group)

- Two tall glasses
- Water
- Food coloring
- Two celery stalks, with leaves
- Carnations (optional)

Safety: *Cut the celery yourself. Do not let children do it.*

In this activity, children will learn that liquids in plants are transported through tiny vertical tubes. Divide the class into small groups. Guide them through the following steps.

1. Put water in both glasses. Add food coloring to one of the glasses.

2. Place a stalk of celery in each glass. (You should cut the bottom inch off each celery stalk just before the student places it in the water.)

3. Leave the celery in the glass overnight.

4. The next day, have the children examine the leaves of the celery for evidence of color.

5. Cut each group's celery stalks in cross sections, and have the children compare the cross section of the celery that was immersed in colored water with that of the other celery.

Discuss with students how the coloring was transported to the upper part of the celery stalk. This experiment can also be done with white carnations. After a period of approximately one day, the flower will take on the color of the liquid in which its stem is placed.

Activity: **Dried Plants**

Materials: (for each student)

- White cornmeal and borax mixture
- Glass jar
- Flower or plant
- Cup with a pouring lip

Ahead of time: Mix six parts of white cornmeal with one part of borax.

Encourage children to find flowers or plants that they would like to save. Assist them with the following steps.

1. Fill the bottom of a glass jar with the cornmeal-borax mixture.

2. Place the flower or plant in the jar, stem up.

3. Slowly pour more of the cornmeal-borax mixture around the flower or plant. Make sure the entire flower is covered by the mixture. Wait two weeks for the flower to completely dry.

4. Gently pour the drying mixture out of the jar, and remove the flower.

Students will enjoy making art projects with their plants or bouquets of dried flowers to give as gifts.

GROWING THINGS

Herbs

ETHNO SCIENCE FACT

In Africa, Zimbabwean traditional healers used a variety of medicinal plants.

LITERATURE

Leavitt, M. *Grena and the Magic Pomegranate.* Minneapolis: Carolrhoda, 1994.

This is the story of a special healer who lives inPomegranate Valley.

Saller, C. *The Bridge Dancers.* Minneapolis: Carolrhoda, 1991.

Maisie helps her mother collect herbs to use in healing the sick. When her sister Callie injures herself, Maisie uses her knowledge of herbal medicines to help Callie.

Wolfson, E. *From the Earth to Beyond the Sky: Native American Medicine.* Boston: Houghton Mifflin Company, 1993.

This book describes the wisdom and lore of the Native American Medicine Men. It tells the story of a people who have lived close to nature and learned many of its secrets.

BACKGROUND INFORMATION

Records of the use of herbs date from ancient Egypt and Biblical times. Herbs were studied for their medical applications and their use in cooking.

Herbs can be grown for cooking, but the medicinal aspect is rarely considered when planting traditional herb gardens. Herb gardens need sunny spots because most of the herbs are native to warm, dry regions.

Herbs are very colorful and can create beautiful gardens. They are noted for their many different shades of gray and blue-green leaves. Although herbs are not known for their blooms, a few, such as lavender, germander, and thyme, are very colorful.

Activity: Herb Garden

Materials:

- Books on herbs and plants used for healing
- Craft sticks
- String
- Herb seeds

Children can investigate the different types of plants and herbs that Native Americans have used to heal sick people. Explain that some of the medicine they are familiar with, such as aspirin, originally came from a plant—willow bark, in the case of aspirin.

After reading the books on herbs and plants used for healing, children may want to plant their own herb garden at school or at home. At school, divide the total garden space into one-foot squares (one for each child). Each square can be roped off, using craft sticks and string. Each child can research one herb he or she would like to grow. Children need to find herbs that can survive in their particular climate. They also need to find out how to take care of their herbs correctly—how much water, sunlight, and nutrients are required. Herbs that might be easy to grow include sage, tarragon, parsley, dwarf basil, thyme, lavender, or mint.

Activity: Herb Hunt

Students can go on an Herb Hunt at a grocery store. If possible, take students on a field trip to a local store that would allow students to wander through the aisles, looking at labels for specific ingredients. Before going to the store, encourage students to research herbs carefully so they can recognize the various names of herbs on product labels.

In the grocery store, have students begin by analyzing the contents of the labels of the following products.

- Natural home remedies—homeopathic vitamins and drugs
- Soap, shampoo, powder, and cosmetics
- Herbal teas
- Actual herbs in the produce section

ETHNO SCIENCE FACT

Amazonians discovered many uses for medicinal plants that play an important role in modern medicine.

A few examples of herbs to look for are angelica, anise, basil, bay leaves, caraway, chamomile, chervil, chives, comfrey, coriander, costmary, cumin, dill, fennel, geranium, lavender, lemon verbena, marigold, marjoram, mint, mustard, nasturtium, oregano, parsley, saffron, sage, santolina, tarragon, and thyme.

Students should be encouraged to find as many products as they can that contain herbs. If it is not possible for the students to go to an actual store to do this activity, bring in a variety of products for the students to analyze in the classroom.

Corn

LITERATURE

Garza, C. *Family Pictures.* Chicago: Children's Book Press, 1990.

This story is written in both English and Spanish. It tells of childhood experiences in Mexico. Making tamales (wrapped in corn husks) is described in careful detail.

Littlesugar, A. *The Spinner's Daughter.* New York: Pippin, 1994.

The is the story of a girl who lives in a Puritan village. In the story, dolls are made out of corn husks.

Monroe, J. and Williamson, R. "The Dove Maidens," *They Dance in the Sky.* Boston: Houghton Mifflin Company, 1987.

This is Pueblo myth of why girls pray to the two Dove Maidens: to stay strong for grinding corn.

BACKGROUND INFORMATION

Many products are made from corn—cornmeal, breakfast foods, hominy, stock feed, synthetic fiber, lacquer, plastics, textile colors, printing inks, cornstarch, corn syrups (glucose), and sugars. Corncobs are ground for a coarse livestock feed. Corn also is used to make polishing powder, insulation, sandblasting materials, man-made fibers, drugs, and solvents. Millions of tons of cornstalks are made into a rubber substitute.

American Indians had many kinds of corn, and there are now more than 1,000 named varieties. The smallest is the golden thumb popcorn plant, about 18 inches high. Some varieties have only eight rows of kernels; others, as many as 48 rows. Colors include white, yellow, red, and blue.

An important ceremony among Native Americans is the "Green Corn Dance." This is common among the Indians of the Southwest. The dance is concerned with agriculture, especially with maize. It involves three phases:

feasting, rejoicing, and worship or thanksgiving. The first Thanksgiving celebration in America was thought to be influenced by this ceremony.

Corn, or maize, was a main food of many Native Americans. Corn belongs to the grass family. Native Americans taught the Pilgrims how to grow corn by planting corn seeds with fish, which fertilized the crop. Corn was cooked many ways. It was boiled or roasted in a fire. Usually, the dry kernels were ground into a powder and made into mush or bread.

Activity: Flat Bread

Materials: (for the teacher)

- Stove or hot plate
- Frying pan
- Cooking spray or oil

Materials: (for the class)

- Flour
- Cornmeal
- Water
- Salt
- Measuring cup
- Bowl
- Jelly or cheese (optional)

Safety: The teacher should do the frying.

Students can make their own flat bread out of a few simple ingredients, following these directions.

1. Measure 2 cups of flour, 2 cups of cornmeal, 2 cups of water and a touch of salt into a bowl. Mix the ingredients.
2. Shape the dough into flat cakes.

Take the student's flat cakes and carefully fry them in a lightly greased pan until golden brown. Students can eat these cakes plain, with jelly, or with melted cheese.

Activity: Cornhusker

Materials: (for each student)

- Three green corn husks
- Scissors
- Craft feathers
- 1 yard of yarn

Students can play a fun game using a "birdie" that they make out of corn husks. The Cornhusker game is very similar to badminton. The birdie is made from corn husks and feathers. The game is played by using the palm of the hand as a paddle. Help the students follow these directions.

1. Lay two corn husks down flat so that they form an X.
2. Repeat step one, so there are now four corn husks forming two X's, one on top of the other.
3. Roll up the third corn husk and lay it in the center of the X.
4. Gather all the ends around the rolled corn husk.
5. Stick feathers into the gathered end.
6. Wrap the yarn around the feathers. Trim the end of the yarn and end of the corn husks.

Ask the students to play this game in pairs. They need to hit the birdie into the air with the palm of their hand. The object of the game is to see who can hit it back and forth the most times in a row without having it fall to the ground.

GROWING THINGS

Peanuts

LITERATURE

Aliki. A *Weed Is a Flower*. New York: Prentice Hall, 1965. This is a life story of the great African American naturalist—George Washington Carver.

BACKGROUND INFORMATION

Peanuts grow in warm or subtropical areas throughout the world. Most of the crops are grown in Africa, Asia, and Indonesia. The largest peanut crops in the United States come from the South, particularly Georgia and Alabama.

Peanuts are high in protein and fatty oils. They are also high in calories. Humans consume peanuts in three forms: the nut, peanut butter, and peanut oil.

A peanut plant has a yellow flowers. The seeds are the edible portion of the plant. Two to four seeds are usually found in a pod, which develops underground for four or five months before it is harvested.

Discussion: *A Weed Is a Flower*

When discussing plants, it is natural to integrate the life and work of George Washington Carver. Discuss his contributions and struggles.

During the American Civil War, in Missouri, a slaveholder by the name of Moses Carver named a motherless child George Washington Carver.

Young Carver was not strong enough to work in the fields, but he did household chores. In the garden, he was good with plants. He had been freed from slavery for several years before he left the Carvers to get an education. In 1896, he graduated with an M. S. degree in Agriculture.

Throughout his 47 years, the great plant scientist made

important strides in scientific agriculture and chemurgy (the industrial use of raw products from plants). He created hundreds of useful products from peanuts and sweet potatoes.

Ten years after his death in Tuskegee on January 5, 1943, Carver's birthplace was dedicated as a national monument. He was known as an instructor, researcher, agricultural chemist, and botanist. He is best known for his work with peanuts.

Activity: Peanut Plants

Materials: (for each child)

- Three raw, unroasted peanuts
- A 6-in. flower pot
- Soil
- Water
- Plastic cup

After studying Carver's life, children can plant and grow their own peanut plants by following the following steps. Carefully explain the importance of proper care of plants.

1. Soak three raw, unroasted peanuts overnight in a plastic cup with water to cover the nut.
2. Fill a 6-inch flower pot with soil to 1 inch below the rim.
3. Plant the peanuts 1 to 1 1/2 inches deep, and cover firmly with soil; but do not pack.
4. Keep the soil moist. Do not overwater. Put the plant where it will get direct sunlight. Try to maintain a temperature of 80 degrees Fahrenheit.
5. Peanuts should sprout within 5–8 days. Continue to keep the plant warm and exposed to direct sunlight.
6. Keep a weekly record of plant growth.

Activity: Peanut Butter

Materials: (for the teacher)

- Blender

Materials: (for the class)

- Roasted, shelled peanuts
- Cooking oil
- Salt
- Bowl
- Measuring cup
- Measuring teaspoon
- Rubber spatula
- Half-teaspoon measure
- Jar with lid
- Crackers, bread, or celery

Have students follow these directions to make their own peanut butter.

1. Measure 2 cups of roasted, shelled peanuts; 2 teaspoons of cooking oil; and 1/2 teaspoon of salt into a bowl.

2. Place the ingredients in a blender and close. Have the teacher push the button to blend.

3. Remove the top. Use a rubber spatula to scrape the mixture from the blender sides to the bottom. Close the top. Have the teacher blend it again until it looks like paste or is easy to spread.

4. Store in a tightly-closed jar in a refrigerator. Stir before serving. (Makes 2 cups of peanut butter)

5. To serve, spread the peanut butter on crackers, bread, or celery.

LITERATURE

Gardiner, J. *Stone Fox.* New York: Harper & Row, 1980.

In this story, Willy wants to help his grandfather, who is sick. One of the things he does is harvest a potato crop.

Smith, M. *Kimi and the Watermelon.* New Zealand: Penguin Books, 1989.

This story is about a Maori family and Kimi, who lovingly tends a watermelon whose ripeness will signal the time for her Uncle Tau's return from the city.

Discussion: Farming

Have children discuss what they know about farming. They can brainstorm a list of words related to agriculture (tractor, irrigation, produce, fertilizer, crops, pests, and harvest).

Activity: Bonkai or Bonsai

Materials: (for each child or group)

- Shallow pan
- Soil
- Small plants
- Small rocks
- Water
- Small mirror (optional)
- Hardy tree seedling (optional)
- Coated wire (optional)

Most Japanese homes have some kind of garden. One type of inside garden is *bonkei,* which is a landscape on a tray. Children can create their own bonkei to keep in the classroom. Start with a shallow pan filled with soil. Keep the arrangement simple. Small plants or small rocks can be used. A small mirror can be used to replicate a pond.

Children can also try to practice the art of *bonsai,* which is the cultivation of dwarf trees. Choose a hardy seedling (pine, fir, or oak), pinch back some of the branches, and use coated wire to train the others to bend into interesting positions. Place the tree in a sunny spot, and water it often. Occasionally, brush some of the dirt away from the top of the roots. This will give the bonsai tree a unique and ancient look.

Activity: Iris

Materials: (for each child)

- Flower pot
- Iris bulb
- Soil
- Water

The iris is a well-loved flower of the Japanese people. In Japan, May is the month of the Iris Festival.

Have each student plant one small iris bulb in a 3/4-inch hole. Keep moist until it sprouts. Put the pot out in the sunshine each day.

Children may enjoy visiting a Japanese garden or a Botanical garden at the conclusion of this activity or unit.

Activity: Potatoes

Materials: (for the teacher)

- Knife

Materials: (for each child)

- Clay pot
- Potato with buds
- Soil
- Measuring cup
- Plate
- Ruler
- Water
- Paper and pencil

Safety: *Do not let children handle the knife.*

Many types of plants can be grown without seeds. It is possible to grow a potato without a seed. Potato plants produce seeds and flowers. Scientists and farmers use the seeds to produce new varieties of potatoes. Potato sprouts grow from the eyes, or buds, on a potato's skin. The white part serves as a food supply for the potato. Each bud can grow into a plant with many potatoes.

ETHNO SCIENCE FACT

A major improvement in farming technology took place in Vietnam c. 1600 B.C. True plows were developed. Cast in bronze, these plows made it possible for larger areas to be planted. Systems of canals and terraces were also in place at this time.

Help children follow these directions for growing potatoes.

1. Fill a clay pot almost full with soil. Put the pot on a plate and water the soil slowly until water overflows.

2. Have the teacher cut off a piece of potato that has a bud.

3. Poke a hole in the soil; make the hole slightly deeper than the size of the potato piece. Bury the piece of potato. Make sure to keep the bud up.

4. Keep the soil moist, but not wet.

5. Record the plant's progress daily. Record carefully the amount of water given and the amount of sunlight the plant receives. Record the growth of the plant (in centimeters) each day.

Allow the children to predict what they think will happen after a week, after two weeks, and so on. They should record their observations and discuss outcomes with the class. Were their predictions accurate? They may want to grow other types of plants and again make predictions, complete the experiment, and validate their results.

Trees

LITERATURE

Edwards, R. *Ring of Tall Trees.* New York: Tambourine, 1993.

A boy and his family are helped by Native Americans and the trickster Raven in their efforts to stop the logging of an old-growth forest.

Giono, J. *The Man Who Planted Trees.* New York: Chelsea Green, 1985.

A Frenchman plants 100 perfect acorns every day and, over his lifetime, reforests a once desolate area in Provence, France. (Students might compare this man's efforts with those of the American Johnny Appleseed.)

Luenn, N. *Song for the Ancient Forest.* New York: Atheneum, 1993.

Raven, the trickster, tells the story about the need to save ancient forests from clear-cutting.

BACKGROUND INFORMATION

A plant is called a tree if it has a woody stem 8 feet or more in height. The stem often has no branches for several feet above the ground. At the top, it has a crown of branches and leaves. It is easy to tell most trees apart. The leaf gives an important clue as to the kind of tree it is. No two kinds of trees have exactly the same shaped leaf. Flowers and seeds also differ with every kind of tree. Trees can be identified by their shape, branching pattern, twigs and buds, and by the texture of their bark.

Activity: Trees

Materials: (for the class)

- Clay pots
- Soil
- Acorns, seeds, or seedlings for trees and other plants
- Water

Children can begin to investigate what types of trees exist throughout various parts of the world. Then students can plant their own trees and compare the growth rates of several different kinds of plants. Do oak trees grow at the same rate that maple trees do? How does the growth rate of trees compare with other plants, such as vegetables or flowers? Do all seeds produce vegetation equally? Children can experiment with different types of seeds and speculate about the reasons why all seeds do not germinate and sprout. By experimenting with the amount of sunlight, soil, and water students can discover the best circumstances under which to develop plants.

Activity: Leaf Prints

Materials: (for each group)

- Paper bag
- Old newspapers
- Fabric paint, or acrylic paint mixed with textile medium
- Rolling pin
- Paper bowl or tray
- Permanent fabric marker
- Plastic trash bag

Materials: (for each child)

- Cardboard
- Prewashed T-shirt
- Sponge paint brush
- Waxed paper

Ahead of time: Cut out 15-in. by 15-in. pieces of waxed paper. Cover tables with newspaper. To facilitate this activity, allow students to use only one color for their prints. Put a different color paint in a paper bowl or tray at each table. Take students on a nature walk. During the walk, encourage children to collect approximately 20 special and unique leaves. They can put the leaves in a paper bag. Once leaves are collected, students need to immediately do leaf prints before the leaves dry out.

Safety: Carefully explain what poison oak, ivy, and sumac look like so these plants can be avoided.

ETHNO SCIENCE FACT

The bark of the Cinchona tree was used by traditional healers in Peru to treat fevers. It is now known as the source of quinine. Quinine was, for many centuries, the only drug effective against malaria, and became popular as a beverage—tonic water.

Have students follow these directions to make leaf prints.

1. Place a piece of cardboard inside a prewashed T-shirt so paint will not bleed through. Lay the T-shirt flat on a table.

2. Choose 5 leaves. Arrange the leaves on the shirt in the location you want to print.

3. Cover the most textured side of the leaf with paint, using sponge paint brushes.

4. Carefully place the leaf on the shirt. Cover it with waxed paper.

5. Use a rolling pin to gently press over the waxed paper. Carefully remove the waxed paper and leaf, and throw them away in a plastic trash bag.

6. Repeat steps 3–5 until all five leaves are used to print. Be careful not to smear the paint.

7. Let shirt dry overnight.

The next day, ask students to identify the leaves on their shirts. Use permanent markers to write the identifying name under each leaf. Have an "I Love Trees" day. Ask everyone to wear their shirts to school (perhaps on Arbor Day or Earth Day).

Activity: Tree Photos

Materials: (for each group)

- Polaroid instant camera
- Markers
- Poster board
- Sketchbook (optional)

Divide the class into groups. If possible, give one camera to each group. Take the class on a nature walk in an area that has a wide variety of trees. Encourage the children to take photos of trees (with and without classmates in the picture). Ask them to write captions for each picture. When everyone returns to the classroom, each group can use the pictures and captions to make a display on poster board. These displays can be placed up on walls throughout the school. (This would make a nice activity to display for open house.)

If it is not possible to take photos, ask each group to take along sketchbooks and draw pictures as they go along. They will still need to make up captions for their sketches to make a display.

Activity: Paperless Fund-raiser

Challenge the students to think of a way to have a paperless fund-raiser. If it is too difficult to do this the first time, students can try to use only recycled paper in their fund-raiser. They may wish to use their profits to buy seedlings or saplings for the school. Students could plan the fund-raiser to coincide with an Arbor Day celebration.

GROWING
THINGS

*Rain
Forests*

LITERATURE

Cherry, L. *The Great Kapok Tree.* New York: Harcourt Brace, 1990.

The author, using Hispanic characters and hints of the Spanish language, uses a simple story line to explain how all living things within the rain forest are valuable and interdependent.

Lewington, A. *Antonio's Rainforest.* Minneapolis: Carolrhoda Books Inc., 1993.

This is the story of Antonio and a Brazilian rain forest. He becomes involved with the issue of using the rain forest to make rubber.

Lippert, M. *The Sea Serpent's Daughter.* Mahwah, New Jersey: Troll Associates, 1993.

This is a Brazilian legend about how night came to the people of the Amazon River Basin rain forest.

BACKGROUND INFORMATION

Tropical rain forests occur in areas that have a lot of rainfall and warm temperatures. These areas are usually near the equator. Northern South America, parts of Central America, much of equatorial Africa, southeastern Asia, the East Indies, and northern Australia have many tropical rain forests. Rain forests are the most complex communities in the world.

Discussion: The Great Kapok Tree

The Great Kapok Tree can be used as a starting point in learning about ecology, the environment, conservation, and even endangered species. This story provides the background to discuss how we, despite our cultural similarities and differences, are also interdependent. Children can discuss ways in which they are connected with other students in the school or with members of their community. Being connected to others is an important concept for children to understand. This concept helps build lasting bridges for communication and mutual respect.

After reading this book, begin to explore student perceptions about the reasons why the great kapok tree was going to be cut down. What was the wood going to be used for? What types of wood grow in the rain forest? How could we find out? These types of questions will lead naturally into the areas of conservation of materials, recycling, protecting our environment, and protecting various plants and animals that are endangered.

Activity: Rain Forest Recipes

As a fun activity, the class can plan and prepare their own "jungle" picnic. Reproduce copies of the Rain Forest Recipes to send home to parents. Encourage the children (and their parents) to bring one of the ingredients to school. After collecting the ingredients, help the children make the recipes to eat as a special part of their discussion on rain-forest products.

Fantastic Fruit Surprise

2 bananas

2 cups orange juice

2 cups pineapple juice

2 cans lemon-lime soft drink

2 pints lemon sherbet

1 can Mandarin oranges

1 can crushed pineapple

Puree 2 soft, ripe bananas in a blender. Add the orange juice, crushed pineapple, oranges, and pineapple juice; and blend together. Just before serving, add the lemon-lime soft drink, and mix well, Put a spoonful of lemon sherbet in each glass, and fill with punch. Makes about 2 quarts.

Forest Mix-Up

2 cups cashew pieces
2 cups broken banana chips
2 cups dried pineapple chunks
1 cup coconut flakes

2 cups peanuts
1 cup sesame seeds
2 cups chocolate chips
1 cup macadamia nuts

Combine the ingredients in a large mixing bowl.
Makes about 4 pounds.

Hot Chocolate Mystery Drink

3 cups milk
1 cup cocoa
1 1/2 cups sugar

3 teaspoons vanilla
whipped topping
nutmeg

3/4 teaspoon cinnamon

In a saucepan, heat milk until hot, but not boiling. In a small bowl mix the cocoa, sugar and cinnamon. Add 2 tablespoons hot milk to the chocolate mixture, stir until smooth. Blend the chocolate mixture into the remaining milk. Remove from heat, add vanilla, and beat with a wire whisk until frothy. To serve, add a spoonful of whipped topping, and a sprinkle of nutmeg to each cup of chocolate. Makes about 3 quarts.

BACKGROUND INFORMATION

Long ago, the Chinese discovered that a thin, wet layer of tiny, interlocking fibers becomes paper when it dries. Today paper comes in thousands of types and grades. Paper and pulp are produced in nearly all countries. The United States, Japan, and Canada are the leading manufacturers of paper. American consumers use nearly 71 million tons of paper a year.

Activity: Papermaking

Materials: (for the teacher)

- Blender

Materials: (for the class)

- Old paper bags
- Old newspapers
- Hot water
- Measuring cup
- Flat pan

- Piece of screen to fit in flat pan
- Rolling pin
- Food coloring (optional)
- Perfume (optional)

Safety: *The teacher should operate the blender.*

To help protect and save trees, children can learn the process of recycling paper by creating their own personal stationery. Help students follow these directions.

1. Tear used paper (paper bags or newspapers) into very tiny pieces.

2. Put torn paper into a blender. Add 2 cups of hot water. Have the teacher blend the paper and water to make pulp. (Try adding food coloring or perfume to your water when you make the pulp.)

3. Pour the pulp into a flat pan. Slide a piece of screen into the bottom of the pan and move it around until it is evenly covered with pulp. Lift the screen out carefully. Hold it level and let it drain for two minutes.

4. Place the screen, pulp side up, on several layers of newspaper. Cover it with another layer of newspaper. Roll over the stack several times with the rolling pin to squeeze out excess water.

5. Carefully remove the top layers of newspaper. Move the screen (and pulp) to more newspaper to dry.

6. When the newspaper is almost dry, peel it off the screen and lay it on more newspaper to finish drying. Allow the paper to dry overnight before using it.

For a class fund-raiser, the children might produce their own paper and decorate it for special occasions. They could also paint the image of endangered animals on the paper and sell it to raise money to help preserve the rain forests around the world. Money can also be donated to help protect various endangered species the children choose to adopt. Children will need to solve the following problems.

- How much paper and water are needed to make enough pulp?

- What exactly will we need to purchase before beginning this project?

- To whom will we sell our decorated paper?

- How much will we charge?

- How will we keep track of our finances?

- How will our money actually be sent and used to help the rain forests and animals?

UNIT 9

light & sound

The Sun

LITERATURE

Dayrell, E. *Why the Sun and the Moon Live in the Sky.* Boston: Houghton Mifflin Co., 1968.

Sun and Moon build a very large house for their friend Water. This story describes what happens in this African folk tale.

McDermott, G. *Arrow to the Sun: A Pueblo Indian Tale.* New York: Viking, 1974.

This is the Pueblo legend that tells of how the spirit of the sun was brought to Earth.

BACKGROUND INFORMATION

The Anasazi Native Americans designed their buildings to make maximum use of solar energy. Often boulders were assembled in a way that gave information about the sun's motion to simulate a calendar. Children should understand that the sun is a star. It is the brightest star in the sky because it is close to Earth, compared to other stars. Sun spots are great storms of hot gases on the surface of the sun. Sunspot observations can help in determining the rate of the sun's rotation.

Activity: Sunspots

Materials: (for the class)

- Binoculars or a small telescope
- White paper
- Large cardboard square
- Marker

Safety: Remind students that they should never look directly at the sun. They should never look into the eyepiece of a telescope or binocular pointed at the sun.

Project the image of the sun with a binocular or small telescope onto a piece of white paper. Use a large cardboard square to cast a shadow on the white paper to improve the projected image's contrast. Have the students mark the circumference of the sun's projected image, and have them mark the sunspots. Have them mark the sunspots daily for the week. Did the sunspots move? Why?

Activity: Sun Prints

Materials: (for each child)

- Construction paper, dark and light
- Scissors
- Tape
- Paper and pencil

Allow students to create sun prints. Have them cut shapes or letters from light-colored construction paper. Then have students tape these pieces to a large sheet of dark-colored construction paper. Set the papers in direct sunlight first thing in the morning. Have the students write predictions about what will happen. At the end of the day, let students peel off the pieces and examine and record the results.

Shadows

LITERATURE

Brown, M. *Shadow*. New York: Aladdin Books, 1982.

This story presents the African legend of how shadows are important to people and how they came to be. The eerie, shifting image of Shadow appears where there is light and fire and a storyteller to bring it to life.

Activities: Shadow Play

Materials:

- Long sheet of butcher paper
- Crayons or markers
- Overhead or slide projector or 100-watt light bulb
- Chalk, a pebble, or a stick
- Paper

Young children can be stimulated by thinking about and playing with shadows. These activities lay a foundation for upper-grade study of daylight astronomy subjects, such as the sun, motion of the earth, sundials, time, and the solar system. Use the following activities.

- Have children explore what kind of shadows various objects make. What objects make the biggest, roundest, or flattest shadows?

- Ask students to work in pairs. Have them use butcher paper and draw around each other's shadows.

- Encourage children to catch a shadow on a hand or a piece of paper.

- Have children play shadow tag.

- Mark a spot on the ground with chalk, a pebble, or a stick. Have children point to the spot with the shadow of a finger. Have them encircle the spot with the shadow of their fingers. Challenge them to find out how far away they can stand and still point with a shadow at the spot on the ground.

- Have children shake shadow hands and touch shadow fingers.

- Let children tell a story using shadows. Use a patch of sunlight for a stage or use a 100-watt light bulb or slide projector, instead of the sun.
- Draw silhouette head portraits of your students, using the light from an overhead projector or a slide projector.

Activity: Shadows

Materials:

- Tape

Take the children outside and have them find out whether shadows are only on the ground or are all over. Have children follow the sun by putting a taped X on a south-facing window and marking the shadow along the wall or floor throughout the day. Mark the shadow of a building, and see if the shadow moves. Will the shadow ever come back to where it was? Ask the children if there are objects that do not have shadows. Find out the answer to this question by experimenting with different objects in t he classroom.

Color

LITERATURE

Chang, C. *The Seventh Sister.* Mahwah, New Jersey: Troll Associates, 1994.

This is a Chinese legend about seven sisters (who make rainbows) and the adventure of Chang and Mei.

Mollel, T. "A Promise to the Sun," *Images.* Lexington, Massachusetts: D. C. Heath and Company, 1995.

This folk tale tells how the sun's light helped the world when a severe drought hit the land of the birds.

BACKGROUND INFORMATION

We see color everywhere. The sky can be blue or black or gray, even reddish or purplish. Soils can be black or brown or gray, even red. Bodies of water look blue or green. Color can give us information. When the green leaves of a plant turn brown, it may be a sign that the plant is sick. It can also be a sign of the season of year, since, in the autumn, leaves of many trees turn brown. The color of a fruit can reveal whether it is ripe. Color depends on light. In fact, it cannot exist apart from light.

Light from the noontime sun looks white. If a ray of white light is aimed at a prism, a broad band of different colors emerges, looking like a rainbow. This color array is called the visible spectrum. White light is a mixture of many different colors. A prism is able to bend light in such a way that the individual colors separate.

From earliest times, the rainbow has delighted and puzzled observers. People invented myths to explain the beautiful arc of multicolored light that appeared after rain. The rainbow is actually a spectrum, formed by sunlight passing through raindrops.

Activity: A Prism

Materials: (for the class or small groups)

- Shallow pan
- Hand mirror
- Water
- White paper

Help students fill a shallow pan with water, and put it in the sun. Have children insert a mirror into the pan and sit it against the side of the pan. Wait for the water to get very smooth. Carefully move the mirror up and down until students see a rainbow on a piece of white paper. Different colors of light have different wavelengths. In this experiment, students take white light apart and separate it into its different colors.

Activity: Color in Markers

Materials: (for each pair of children)

- Coffee filters (cone shaped)
- Scissors
- Washable markers in a variety of colors and brands
- Drinking glasses
- Water

Students can further explore the concept of colors by completing the following experiment. Students will see that the inks in marking pens are often combinations of several colored dyes. Guide students through the following steps to test markers.

1. Use one coffee filter for each marker to be tested.

2. On one side of the filter, make two cuts, approximately 1/2 inch apart, from the edge of the filter toward the center. Fold back this portion. Do the same on the other side of the filter and hang it on the side of a glass.

3. Make a large, heavy marker dot approximately 1 inch up from the bottom of the filter.

4. Fill a glass with water so that the water does not quite reach the marker dot. (The marker is water soluble so, if the dot is immersed in the water, the ink will dissolve into the water.)

The separation process takes about 20 minutes. Based on children's prior experiments with mixing colors to make other colors, ask them to guess what new colors might be formed from each marker. Then discuss the results.

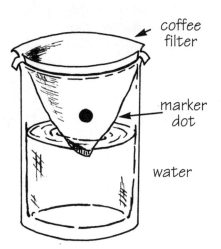

- What color marker contains the most colors?

- Which colors or types of markers do not separate?

- Which colors move highest on the test strips?

Change the temperature of the water. How does temperature affect the separation process?

LITERATURE

Music

Greenfield, E. *Honey, I Love and Other Love Poems.* New York: Thomas Y. Crowell, 1978.

This is a collection of sixteen poems told through the feelings and impressions of a young black child. These poems could easily be put to music or a rhythmic beat.

Isadora, R. *Ben's Trumpet.* New York: Greenwillow Books, 1979.

This is the story of a young boy in the 1920s who sits on his fire escape, longing to play jazz. It incorporates the difficulties he has in not owning an instrument and the shame he feels when his friends ridicule him.

Mattox, C. *Shake It to the One That You Love the Best: Plays, Songs, and Lullabies from Black Musical Traditions.* Nashville, Tennessee: Warren-Mattox, 1989.

This is a collection of African American plays, songs, and lullabies.

Discussion: Ben's Trumpet

Ben's Trumpet can be used to integrate music and sound within a multicultural setting. Tell the students that this story is about a boy named Ben, who plays an imaginary instrument. Ask students if they play any musical instruments or if any members of their families play instruments. Discuss the instruments that they know. Can they demonstrate to the class how they would play certain instruments? Encourage the students to role-play and pretend to play a variety of instruments. This will be a great warm-up activity before you read the book. After reading the book, discuss the plot of the story. Discuss Ben and how he might have felt after he played a real trumpet. If possible, try to ask a real trumpet player to come and perform for your class. If this is not possible, try to at least have a video or recording of someone playing trumpet music. Let the children listen to a variety of recorded instruments. Challenge them to identify the instruments they hear.

Activity: Radio Play

Materials: (for the class)

- A play
- Sound-effects materials

In cooperative-learning groups, have students find a play suitable for a short "radio" play. Ask them to gather materials for sound effects. They should practice the play until it can be presented smoothly. Tape a five-minute portion of the radio play with the sound effects.

Activity: Montage

Materials: (for the class)

- Discarded magazines
- Poster board
- Glue

Help students create an art montage of things that make sounds. Let them glue magazine pictures on a poster-board display for the room. Encourage them to be as diverse and as creative as possible.

Activity: Sounds

Materials: (for the teacher)

- A collection of materials that make noise, such as tissue paper, wood, carpeting, glass
- A screen to block children's view
- Chart paper
- Marker

Create a sound guessing game. Borrow a screen and make a chart listing the materials that you will use to make sound. Tell listeners that this activity will determine how well they are able to guess the source of a sound. Behind the screen, use each item to make a sound. Create a graph showing the correct number of responses for each item.

Vibrations

LITERATURE

Walker, M. *Ty's One-Man Band.* New York: Four Winds, 1980.

In this African American story, Ty meets Andro who makes beautiful music with some very interesting objects.

BACKGROUND INFORMATION

Every kind of sound is produced by vibration. The sound source may be a violin, an automobile horn, or a barking dog. Whatever it is, some part of it is vibrating while it is producing sound. The vibrations from the source disturb the air in such a way that sound waves are produced. These waves travel out in all directions, expanding in balloonlike fashion from the source of the sound. If the waves happen to reach someone's ear, they set up vibrations that are perceived as sound.

Sound depends on three things. There must be a vibrating source to set up sound waves, a medium (such as air) to carry the waves, and a receiver to detect them.

Activity: High and Low Sounds

Materials:

- Double bass and violin (or close-up pictures and recordings of them)

Tell students that they can make low sounds and high sounds. Encourage them to speak in deep voices. Next, ask them to speak in very high, squeaky voices. Ask them to explain how they are able to do that. How do they make sounds? What are vocal cords? Where are they? Tell the students that the vocal cords in their throats help them make these sounds. Long, thick cords make low sounds; and short, thin cords make high sounds. Students can compare the long, thick strings on a double bass in an orchestra with the short, thin strings of a violin. A double bass can make deep sounds. A violin can make higher sounds.

Activity: Sound Conductors

Materials: (for each group)

- Balloons
- Water
- Watch or small clock

Help children follow these directions.

1. Blow up a balloon and hold it next to your ear. Hold a ticking watch on the other side of the balloon.
2. Now fill another balloon with water and hold it next to your ear with the watch.

Discuss which balloon makes the sound louder? Why? (Sound travels 5 times faster through water than it does through air. The sound will be louder through the water-filled balloon.)

Activity: Voice Picture

Materials: (for each group)

- Balloon
- Cardboard tube
- Rubber band
- Glue
- Aluminum foil
- Flashlight
- Black paper (optional)

To see a picture of a voice, have students try this.

1. Cut off the neck area of a balloon. Discard the neck.
2. Stretch the rest of the balloon tightly over the end of a cardboard tube. Use a rubber band to hold the balloon in place.
3. Glue a small square of aluminum foil onto the balloon skin.
4. Shine a flashlight onto the foil at an angle so that you can see a spot of light reflected onto the wall or a sheet of black paper.
5. Speak into the open end of the tube. Try high and low sounds, as well as loud and soft sounds. Watch the spot of light as it vibrates to your voice.

Drums

LITERATURE

Achebe, C. *The Drum.* New York: Fourth Dimension, 1977.

This is a Nigerian folk tale that describes the adventures of Tortoise, a young boy, and a magic drum. When beating the drum, the young boy can summon up a sumptuous banquet. As a result, he has several interesting adventures with members of the animal kingdom.

Bryan, A. *The Cat's Purr.* New York: Atheneum, 1985.

In this African American folklore, Rat and Cat were good friends until Cat got a drum that played beautiful music.

Activity: **Drums**

Materials: (for each child or small group)

- Empty coffee can with two plastic lids
- Construction paper
- Markers

Ahead of time: *Take the metal lids off both ends of the coffee cans and replace them with plastic lids.*

Native American drums were used in ceremonies and celebrations. Your class can make them from coffee cans. Have students decorate the cans with construction paper and markers. Then let children play the drums. You may want to save the drums to use again in the next activity.

Activity: **Taiko Drums**

Materials: (for each child or small group)

- Empty coffee can with two plastic lids
- Chopsticks
- Masking tape

Ahead of time: *Take the metal lids off both ends of the coffee cans and replace them with plastic lids. Or use the cans from the previous activity.*

In Japan, taiko drums are used. Children can make them, too. Have children put masking tape balls on two chopsticks. Then have them beat the drums with rapid, strong beats.

Activity: **Drum Sounds**

Materials: (for the teacher)

- Videotapes or recordings of sounds made by different drums
- Player for videotape or recordings

Play the sounds of drums such as timpani, snare, bass, bongo, and steel drums. Students can learn to identify each drum by its unique sound.

Conclusion

We are a multicultural society. It is important to learn how others live, think, and act. Due to the power of satellites, we are connected to one another around the world closer than ever before. We are all quickly affected by events, disasters, and ideas from places we may never actually visit. Mountains, oceans, differing languages, and lack of transportation were all once considered barriers to communication and understanding. Not anymore! Through computers, fax machines, airplanes, and even radar, we are now able to be a part of an interconnected multicultural community. Children need to appreciate the wonderful differences among people around the world, as well as learn how they are the same.

Cultural diversity among children will always exist. Our job is not to eliminate diversity, but to recognize it and use it to the educational advantage of children. When learners are provided opportunities to negotiate their cultural backgrounds, interests, and cognitive styles in the learning environment, they are more inclined to experience academic success.

The concepts discussed in this book provide examples of what can be taught and integrated within a typical elementary science curriculum. A multicultural connection can be made within these areas. Children from a variety of ethnic backgrounds can be touched by the literature and activities. The history and culture of students can be valuable when making curriculum decisions, adapting pedagogy, and increasing achievement in science education.

Teacher Resources

Science References

Addison-Wesley. *A World of Mathematics, Science, and Technology: Wall Chart.* New York: Addison-Wesley Publishing, Co. Inc., 1992.

Basak, Susan. *Science Is . . .* Ontario: Scholastic, Canada Ltd., 1991.

Cole H. *We're Shaking and Quaking: Science Grasp 1993,* Michigan: Upjohn Co., 1993.

Lorbeer, G. and Nelson, L. *Science Activities for Children.* Wm. C. Brown Publishers, 1992.

Smith, E. Blackmer, M. & S. Schlichting, *Super Science Source Book.* Idea Factory, 1987.

Multicultural References

Appleton, N. *Cultural Pluralism in Education.* New York: Longman Press, 1983.

Banks, J. and C. Banks. *Multicultural Education.* Boston: Allyn and Bacon, 1993.

Bennett, C. I. *Comprehensive Multicultural Education: Theory and Practice* (2nd. Ed.) Boston: Allyn and Bacon, 1990.

Boston Public Schools. *Drawing on Diversity: A Handbook of Effective Teaching Techniques for the Multicultural Classroom.* Boston: 1989.

Grossman, H. *Special Education in a Diverse Society.* Needham, Massachusetts: Allyn and Bacon, 1994.

Grossman, H. *Teaching in a Diverse Society.* Boston: Allyn and Bacon, 1995.

Ramirez, M., & Castaneda, A. *Cultural Democracy, Bicognitive Development and Education.* New York: Academic Press, 1974.

Rakow, S. and A. Bermudez. "Science Is 'Ciencia': Meeting the Needs of Hispanic American Students," *Science Education,* Vol. 77 (6) (1993), pp. 669–683.

Selin, H. "Science Across Culture." *The Science Teacher,* (March, 1993), pp. 38–43.

Tharp, R. G. "Psychocultural variables and constants: Effects on teaching and learning in schools." *American Psychologist,* Vol. 44 (1989), pp. 349–359.

Villegas, A. M. "Culturally Responsive Pedagogy for the 1990s and Beyond." Trends and Issues Paper No. 6. Washington, D C: ERIC Clearinghouse on Teacher Education, 1991.

Aardema, V. *Bringing the Rain to Kapiti Plain.* New York: Dial Books for Young Readers, 1981.

Aardema, V. *Why Mosquitoes Buzz in People's Ears.* New York: Dial Books for Young Readers, 1975.

Achebe, C. *The Drum.* New York: Fourth Dimension, 1977.

Ai-Ling , L. *Yeh-Shen: A Cinderella Story from China.* New York: Philomel Books, 1982.

Aliki. *A Weed Is a Flower.* New York: Simon & Schuster, 1965.

Argueta, M. *Magic Dogs of the Volcanoes.* San Francisco: Children's Book Press, 1990.

Arkhurst, J. "Why Spider Lives in Ceilings," *The Adventures of Spider.* Boston: Little, Brown and Company, 1964.

Aruego, J. and A. Aruego. *A Crocodile's Tale.* New York: Scholastic Book Services, 1972.

Ata, T. *Baby Rattlesnake.* Chicago: Children's Book Press, 1989.

Baker, J. *Window.* New York: Greenwillow, 1991.

Baylor, B. *Hawk, I'm Your Brother.* New York: Scribner's, 1976.

Baylor, B. *When Clay Sings.* New York: Atheneum, 1981.

Beatty, P. *Digging for China.* Parsippany, New Jersey: Silver, Burdett & Ginn Inc., 1989.

Belpre, P. "The Legend of the Hummingbird," *Tales from Here and There.* Lexington, Massachusetts: D. C. Heath and Company, 1995.

Bierhorst, J. *The Monkey's Haircut and Other Stories Told by the Maya.* New York: Morrow, 1986.

Binch, C. *Gregory Cool.* New York: Dial, 1994.

Bonnici, P. *The First Rains.* London: Mantra Publishing Ltd., 1984.

Brown, M. *Shadow.* New York: Aladdin Books, 1982.

Bryan, A. *The Cat's Purr.* New York: Atheneum, 1985.

Bush, T. *Three at Sea.* New York: Crown, 1994.

Children's Literature

Caduto, M. and J. Bruchac. "Moth, the Fire Dancer," *Keepers of the Night.* Golden, Colorado: Fulcrum Publishing, 1994.

Carpenter, F. "The Shah Weaves a Rug," *The Elephant's Bathtub.* New York: Doubleday, 1962.

Chang, C. *The Seventh Sister.* Mahwah, New Jersey: Troll Associates, 1994.

Cherry, L. *The Great Kapok Tree.* New York: Harcourt Brace Jovanovich, 1990.

Chief Seattle. *Brother Eagle, Sister Sky: A Message from Chief Seattle.* New York: Dial, 1991.

Cohen, C. *Mud Pony.* New York: Scholastic Inc., 1988.

Coutant, H. *First Snow.* New York: Random House, Inc., 1974.

Cruz, M. *Yagua Days.* New York: Dial, 1987.

Dayrell, E. *Why the Sun and the Moon Live in the Sky.* Boston: Houghton Mifflin Company, 1968.

Demi. *Demi's Secret Garden.* New York: Holt, 1993.

de Paola, T. *The Legend of the Bluebonnet.* New York: G. P. Putnam's Sons, 1983.

de Paola, T. *Bill and Pete.* New York: Putnam & Grosset, 1992.

DuBois, W. *The Twenty-One Balloons.* New York: Puffin, 1975.

Dunn K. and R. Dunn. *Teaching Students Through Their Individual Learning Styles.* Reston, Virginia: National Council of Principals, 1978.

Dupre, R. *Agassu: Legend of the Leopard King.* Minneapolis: Carolrhoda Books, 1993.

Edmiston, J. *Little Eagle Lots of Owls.* Boston: Houghton Mifflin Company, 1993.

Edwards, R. *Ring of Tall Trees.* New York: Tambourine, 1993.

Feelings, M. *Moja Means One: Swahili Counting Book.* New York: Dial Books for Young Readers, 1971.

Ferreira, F. *Feathers Like a Rainbow: An Amazon Indian Tale.* New York: Harper & Row, 1989.

Fife, D. *The Empty Lot.* Boston: Little, Brown and Co., 1991.

Finsand, M. *The Town That Moved.* Minneapolis: Carolrhoda Books, 1983.

Fuja, A. *Fourteen Hundred Cowries and Other African Tales.* New York: Lothrop, 1971.

Gardiner, J. *Stone Fox.* New York: Harper & Row, 1980.

Garland, S. and T. Kivchi. *The Lotus Seed.* San Diego: Harcourt Brace Jovanovich, 1993.

Garza, C. *Family Pictures.* Chicago: Children's Book Press, 1990.

Gates, F. *Owl Eyes.* New York: Lothrop, 1994.

George, J. *Julie of the Wolves.* New York: Harper & Row, 1972.

George, J. *The Talking Earth.* New York: HarperCollins, 1983.

George, J. *Who Really Killed Cock Robin? An Ecological Mystery.* New York: HarperCollins, 1991.

Ginsburg, M. *How the Sun Was Brought Back to the Sky.* New York: Macmillan, 1975.

Giono, J. *The Man Who Planted Trees.* New York: Chelsea, 1985.

Gissing, V. *Joshua and the Big Wave.* E. Sussex, England: Macdonald Young Books, Ltd., 1989.

Goble, P. *Dream Wolf.* New York: Bradbury Press, 1990.

Goble, P. *The Girl Who Loved Wild Horses.* New York: Macmillan, 1982.

Goble, P. *The Great Race of the Birds and Animals.* New York: Bradbury, 1985.

Goble, P. *The Lost Children: The Boys Who Were Neglected.* New York: Bradbury, 1993.

Greenfield, E. *Honey, I Love and Other Love Poems.* New York: Thomas Y. Crowell, 1978.

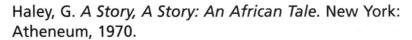

Haley, G. *A Story, A Story: An African Tale.* New York: Atheneum, 1970.

Harill, J. *Sato and the Elephants.* New York: Lothrop, 1993.

Heath, S. B. *Ways with Words: Language, Life, and Work in Communities and Classrooms.* New York: Cambridge University Press, 1983.

Henry, M. *Brighty of the Grand Canyon.* New York: Macmillan, 1991.

Holcroft, A. *Chen Li and the River Spirit.* London: Hodder and Stoughton, 1991.

Houston, J. *Frozen Fire.* New York: McElderry Books, 1977.

Houston, J. *Long Claws: An Arctic Adventure.* New York: McElderry Books, 1981.

Hoyt-Goldsmith, D. and L. Migdale. *Pueblo Storyteller.* New York: Holiday, 1991.

Isadora, R. *Ben's Trumpet.* New York: Greenwillow Books, 1979.

Ishii, M. *The Tongue-Cut Sparrow.* New York: Lodestar/ E. P. Dutton, 1986.

Joseph, L. *Jasmine's Parlour Day.* New York: Lothrop, Lee & Shepard Books, 1994.

Keeler, K. *Little Fox.* New York: Macmillan, 1936.

Kerr-Wilson, B. *Turtle and the Island.* London: Frances Lincoln, 1990.

Kloben, H. and B. Day. *Hey, I'm Alive!* London: Curtis Brown, Ltd., 1963.

Leavitt, M. *Grena and the Magic Pomegranate.* Minneapolis: Carolrhoda Books, 1994.

Lessac, F. *My Little Island.* New York: Harper & Row Publishers, 1984.

Lester, J. *How Many Spots Does a Leopard Have? And Other Tales.* New York: Scholastic Inc., 1989.

Lewin, H. and L. Kopper. *A Shell on the Beach.* London: Hamish Hamilton, 1989.

Lewington, A. *Antonio's Rainforest*. Minneapolis: Carolrhoda Books, 1993.

Lewis, T. *Hill of Fire*. New York: Harper & Row, 1971.

Lippert, M. *The Sea Serpent's Daughter*. Mahwah, New Jersey: Troll Associates, 1993.

Littlesugar, A. *The Spinner's Daughter*. New York: Pippin, 1994.

Luenn, N. *Song for the Ancient Forest*. New York: Atheneum, 1993.

Mattox, C. *Shake It to the One That You Love the Best: Play, Songs and Lullabies from Black Musical Traditions*. Nashville, Tennessee: Warren-Mattox, 1989.

Mayo, G. "Coyote Makes the Constellations," *Tell Me a Tale*. Lexington, Massachusetts: D. C. Heath and Company, 1995.

McDermott, G. *Anansi the Spider*. New York: Henry Holt & Co., 1972.

McDermott, G. *Arrow to the Sun: A Pueblo Indian Tale*. New York: Viking, 1974.

McKissack, P. *Mirandy and Brother Wind*. New York: Knopf, 1988.

Mendez, P. *The Black Snowman*. New York: Scholastic Inc., 1989.

Merrill, J. and F. Cooper. *The Girl Who Loved Caterpillars*. New York: Putnam, 1992.

Mike, J. and C. Reasoner. *Opossum & the Great Firemaker*. Mahwah, New Jersey: Troll Associates, 1993.

Millhoff, K., A. Griese, A. Borgo, et. al. *Gift from the Storm and Other Stories of Children Around the World*. Honesdale, Pennsylvania: Boyds Mills Press, 1993.

Mollel, T. *The King and the Tortoise*. New York: Clarion, 1993.

Mollel, T. "A Promise to the Sun," *Images*. Lexington, Massachusetts: D. C. Heath and Company, 1995.

Monroe, J. and R. Williamson. "The Dove Maidens," *They Dance in the Sky*. Boston: Houghton Mifflin Company, 1987.

Morgan, W. *Navajo Coyote Tales.* Santa Fe, New Mexico: Ancient City Press, 1988.

Newton, D. *Spider and the Sky God.* Mahwah, New Jersey: Troll Associates, 1993.

Newton, P. *The Five Sparrows.* New York: Atheneum, 1982.

Newton, P. *The Stonecutter.* New York: G. P. Putnam's Sons, 1990.

O'Dell, S. *The Black Pearl.* Boston: Houghton Mifflin Company, 1967.

Palacios, A. *The Hummingbird King.* Mahwah, New Jersey: Troll Associates, 1993.

Palacios, A. *The Llama's Secret.* Mahwah, New Jersey: Troll Associates, 1993.

Polacco, P. *Rechenka's Eggs.* New York: Philomel Books, 1988.

Politi, L. *Song of the Swallows.* New York: Macmillan, 1948.

Porte, B. and D. Ruff. *"Leave That Cricket Be, Alan Lee."* New York: Greenwillow, 1993.

Rafe, M. *The Boy Who Lived with Seals.* New York: Putnam Publishing Group, 1993.

Reasoner, C. *The Magic Amber.* Mahwah, New Jersey: Troll Associates, 1994.

Reasoner, C. and J. Mike. *Opossum and the Great Firemaker.* Mahwah, New Jersey: Troll Associates, 1993.

Roadelberger, F. and V. Groschoff. *African Wildlife.* New York: The Viking Press, 1965.

Roy, R. *A Thousand Pails of Water.* New York: Random House, Inc., 1978.

Ryder, J. *Winter Whale.* New York: William Morrow, 1991.

Saller, C. *The Bridge Dancers.* Minneapolis: Carolrhoda Books, 1991.

Selden, G. *Cricket in Times Square.* New York: Farrar, Straus & Giroux, 1960.

Sharma, P. "The Criticism of the Monkey," *Tell Me a Tale.* Lexington, Massachusetts: D. C. Heath and Company, 1995.

Shippen, K. *Lightfoot.* New York: Viking Press, 1953.

Siy, A. *The Eeyou: People of Eastern James Bay.* New York: Dillon Press, Inc., 1993.

Smith, M. *Kimi and the Watermelon.* New Zealand: Penguin Books, 1989.

Sobol, R. and J. Sobol. *Seal Journey.* New York: Cobblehill, 1993.

Sperry, A. "Ghost of the Lagoon," *Fast As the Wind.* Boston: Houghton Mifflin Company, 1993.

Stolz, M. *Storm in the Night.* New York: HarperCollins Publisher, 1988.

Taylor, T. *The Cay.* New York: Doubleday, 1969.

Ullman, J. *Banner in the Sky.* New York: HarperCollins, 1954.

Vizenor, G. "Almost a Whole Trickster," *A Gathering of Flowers,* Joyce Carol Thomas. New York: HarperCollins, 1990.

Walker, A. "Why Did the Balinese Chicken Cross the Road?" *Living by the Word.* San Diego: Harcourt Brace Jovanovich, 1988.

Walter, M. *Brother to the Wind.* New York: Lothrop, Lee & Shepard Books, 1985.

Walker, M. *Ty's One-Man Band.* New York: Four Winds, 1980.

Wartski, M. *A Boat to Nowhere.* Louisville, Kentucky: Westminster John Knox Press, 1980.

White Deer of Autumn. *The Great Change.* Oregon: Beyond Words Publishing, 1992.

Wilkins, V. and G. McLean. *Abena and the Rock.* Camberley, England: Tamarind Ltd., 1991.

Wisniewski, D. *Rain Player.* New York: Lothrop, 1992.

Wolfson, E. *From the Earth to Beyond the Sky: Native American Medicine.* Boston: Houghton Mifflin Company, 1993.

Wolkstein, D. *8,000 Stones: A Chinese Folktale.* New York: Doubleday, 1972.

Yashima, T. *Crow Boy.* New York: Puffin, 1976.

Yep, L. "The Magical Horse," *Tell Me a Tale.* Lexington, Massachusetts: D. C. Heath and Company, 1995.

Yep, L. *Sea Glass.* New York: Harper & Row, 1979.

Yep, L. *The Shell Woman and the King: A Chinese Folktale.* New York: Dial, 1993.

Yolen, J. and E. Young. *The Girl Who Loved the Wind.* New York: Harper Trophy, 1987.

Yolen, J. *Sky Dogs.* San Diego: Harcourt Brace Jovanovich, 1990.

Yoshiko, U. *The Rooster Who Understood Japanese.* New York: Scribner's, 1976.

Young, E. *The Rooster's Horns.* New York: Philomel Books, 1978.